IGNITE
YOUR LIFE

14 POWERFUL THINGS
THAT HAPPEN WHEN YOU PRAY

FRANKIE MAZZAPICA

WHITAKER
HOUSE

IGNITE YOUR LIFE
14 Powerful Things That Happen When You Pray

Celebration Church of The Woodlands
6565 Research Forest Drive | The Woodlands, TX 77381
woodlandscelebration.com
frankiemazzapica.com

ISBN: 979-8-88769-098-8 | eBook ISBN: 979-8-88769-099-5
Printed in Colombia
© 2024 by Frankie Mazzapica

Whitaker House
1030 Hunt Valley Circle | New Kensington, PA 15068
www.whitakerhouse.com

Library of Congress Control Number: 2023946693

1 2 3 4 5 6 7 8 9 10 11 ⨀ 31 30 29 28 27 26 25 24

DEDICATION

Allie, you are my heartbeat. I'm as crazy about you as I was on the day we met. I love our hugs and our kisses. You and I share a bond that cannot be broken and a love that cannot be restrained. I want to spend every day with you. You make life wonderful.

Preslee, you have exceeded all expectations. You're beautiful, strong, tender, and extraordinarily perceptive. Your wisdom over the years has taught me many lessons. You've always hidden Scriptures in your heart. You are a woman of prayer who walks with the Lord.

Luke, you're better than me in every way. You've overcome every obstacle you've had to face. Your strength runs deep. You never hesitate to say, "I love you," and when you say it, we feel it. You're quick to raise your hands in worship. Like David, you're a man after His own heart.

Kate, everyone celebrates you. You're intelligent, you're a leader, and you care for all others deeply. You'll always be successful at whatever you do. You love to pray, and for that reason, you are a source of strength. You'll bring joy wherever you go, just as you have for our family.

To each of you, I challenge you to always pray with passion, as it determines the course of your life. Short prayers are always powerful, long prayers are the secret to intimacy, and worship changes the atmosphere. In all you do, serve the Lord well. Nothing else matters.

CONTENTS

FOREWORD

Frankie Mazzapica is the esteemed pastor of Celebration Church in The Woodlands, Texas. I have known and worked with Frankie for many years and consider him to be a dear friend and an inspiring minister of the gospel. His knowledge of Scripture and insightful perspectives are not only appreciated by the members of his congregation but are respected throughout the Christian community. He is a believer in and witness to the power of prayer, and this book, *Ignite Your Life: 14 Powerful Things That Happen When You Pray*, is the culmination of his many years of experience.

Prayer is an act of faith, and, as we see throughout the Bible, God is moved by our faith. On more than one occasion, Jesus attributed the miracles He worked to the faith held by the person who received the miracle. Faith can move mountains, and it surely moves the heart of God. When we pray, it is our faith that causes healing to flow, angels to act, and God to move on our behalf. Heaven responds to our prayers, and that is why it is so important that prayer be an essential part of our daily lives.

I have often spoken about the fact that I begin each day speaking to God. I ask Him to search my heart, guide my steps, protect my family, and cause all my efforts to succeed. One of the best prayers that we could ever pray is, "God, not my will, but Your will be done." If you will stay open to His direction and follow your heart, God will guide your steps and protect you.

Throughout the fourteen chapters of this book, Frankie will demonstrate how the power of prayer can affect every aspect of your life. When you are facing overwhelming challenges, prayer can cause angels to intervene, the mouths of lions to be shut, and the tide of the battle to turn in your favor. When you feel alone, prayer can help you to sense God's presence, know that all of heaven is behind you, and help you to hear His voice. Prayer can change your family. It can protect and strengthen those you love and turn conflict into peace. It is through prayer that you gain wisdom, make good choices, and avoid turmoil.

Prayer is powerful and can change everything for the better. I am confident that if you read this book with an open heart, accept the principles in it, and make prayer a priority, your life will never be the same. You will live with more confidence and joy, and you will see the blessings of God in every part of your life.

—*Joel Osteen*
Lakewood Church, Houston, Texas

INTRODUCTION

C. S. Lewis once said, "If we find ourselves with a desire that nothing in this world can satisfy, the most probable explanation is that we were made for another world."[1] You were created to live a life in which you experience the incomparable, all-powerful, loving presence of God just as close as the shirt on your back. When you are in a relationship with Jesus, He introduces Himself in ways that are too wonderful for words. The joy is so deep, it cannot be shaken by circumstances.

---

1. C. S. Lewis, *Mere Christianity* (New York: HarperOne, 2015), 136.

We are spiritual beings who have a temporary physical experience. Yet we do not have to wait till we walk streets of gold to walk closely with the Lord; we can enjoy Him now while we walk today's dusty roads during our short stay on earth. At this present time, we are able to learn to clearly hear the voice of God and relay to others the message of grace and hope. We can become a conduit for His power to flow out of to heal the sick, comfort the brokenhearted, and lead them to a place called peace. As our relationship with Jesus becomes more precious than all other things, we are given full assurance that we are living a life of significance that is guaranteed to make an eternal impact.

You were born for more than just to be deemed successful, make money, and fill your life with pleasure. Scriptures reveal that the Lord intends to bless you in every way, but His intentions go far beyond your hopes and dreams. You've been invited to partner with and to be empowered by the Holy Spirit to effectively make a lasting impression that will compel others to devote their lives to worshipping and serving the Lord. It requires great trust to live out the plans set before you. All who are courageous to take that step of faith live a life continually witnessing the power of God. Thus far, you may not have even noticed that you have already been used on multiple occasions to bless and encourage those around you. However, there are levels of impact, and the most significant and lasting impact can only be made while partnering with the almighty God.

"You have a great future ahead of you!" are the words we heard in our youth.

As the years go on, burdens and responsibilities tend to dampen our expectations. Consequently, we begin to think that we've reached our full potential, that the amount of joy we have today is all we should expect in the future. To encourage ourselves, we look forward to believing that when the current season passes, we will be firmly situated to live the life we've always wanted. Yet the following seasons feel just as grueling as the previous ones.

In New York City, there is a massive statue depicting the ancient Greek Titan Atlas carrying the world on his shoulders. St. Patrick's Cathedral is directly across the street. Inside there is a statue of the boy Jesus entitled *Holy Child of Earth and Heaven* who holds the world in the palm of his hands. Everything depends on who we depend on. We can carry our burdens and dreams on our own backs, fully aware that we're not strong enough, or we can trust that, when we are in a relationship with Jesus, our life will exceed all our expectations.

A. W. Tozer once said, "Every man is as full of the Spirit as he wants to be. Make your heart a vacuum and the Spirit will rush in to fill it."[2] All who draw near testify to a love beyond human explanation and a sense of peace that exceeds anything they're able to understand.

---

2. A. W. Tozer, *Man: The Dwelling Place of God: What it Means to Have Christ Living in You*, rev. ed. (Chicago: Moody, 1997), 39, Kindle.

In your pursuit, the presence of God will *Ignite Your Life* in a supernatural way that only prayer can provoke. Within the following pages, your faith will grow, and your anticipation will rise as you discover *14 Powerful Things That Happen When You Pray.*

1

PRAYER TURNS THE TIDE OF YOUR BATTLE

The very day I call for help, the tide of battle turns.
—Psalm 56:9 (TLB)

David was familiar with fear. As a young boy, he encountered lions or bears that would grab a lamb from his father's flock of sheep. Rather than stand paralyzed, he pursued the predator with a club and rescued the lamb from its mouth. If the beast rose against him, he caught it by the jaw and clubbed it to death. By the time David took his stance in front of Goliath, fear was so familiar that it was comfortable. After responding to Goliath's battlefield insults, David ran toward Goliath and selected a stone from his bag. He struck down the Philistine using only a sling and a stone. David then used Goliath's own sword to cut off the giant's head. (See 1 Samuel 17.)

When David was an adult, the troops he commanded would continually return victorious from war. Israel's streets would flood with people singing songs about the tens of thousands David had killed. (See 1 Samuel 18:6–7). David knew how to handle his fear.

In Psalm 56, we find David in a different kind of crisis, one less direct. This time, fear was overtaking him. As a king, he was surrounded by advisors who were really adversaries who twisted his words as they planned to sabotage his reign. They were meeting together to perfect their plans to remove him from the throne and cast him out as an outcast, never to return. They would take great pleasure in killing him.

This time, he wasn't a brave warrior wielding a sword. He was simply a man wondering and weeping. He faced conflict from every direction, with external battles and internal fear. As David felt ridiculed, attacked, and betrayed, he became aware of what God was doing at that very moment. In Psalm 56:9 (TLB), he wrote, "*The very day I call for help, the tide of the battle turns.*"

We will never understand the whole meaning of this short verse, although it is abundantly clear that God is for us. He is for us when the tide of the battle rages against us. He was for us even before the world was made. He was for us when He allowed His only Son to be smitten as the full weight of our sin was upon Him. He is for us when we are not even thinking about Him. He is for us with all the omnipotence of His love, inviting us to seek His face. He is eternally for us. He who turns the hearts of man, directs the wind, and tells the wave where to stop is for us. *"If God is for us, who can ever be against us?"* (Romans 8:31). It is joyful knowing that the King of Kings is on our side. David witnessed how prayer causes enemies to scatter, and so he praises God:

> *This one thing I know: God is for me! I am trusting God—oh, praise his promises! I am not afraid of anything mere man can do to me!* (Psalm 56:9–12 TLB)

There's no way to recall all our thoughts and emotions, but our Father in heaven has recorded every detail of every day we've lived since the moment we were born. Each time you have faced storms resulting in tears, a bottle from heaven was gently pressed against your cheek so not one was lost. Tears are precious to the Lord. (See Psalm 56:8.)

A friend of ours has a daughter named Christina, who was active in theater in high school. There was a kid named Zach who made it his goal to antagonize her. He took pleasure in ridiculing her in front of the class by mocking everything she did and said. Not able to compete with his loud voice and strong personality, she could only sit there and take it. To make the situation all the more painful, her friends would also smirk and laugh, never coming to her defense. Her friends were likely fearful that if they did not side with him, he would redirect his attack toward them.

At the end of the school year, Christina's teachers asked the students to sing on stage in front of the class. Their performance would carry the weight of their final grade. For months leading up to the day of the performance, Zach promised to be in the front row so he could record her with his phone and post the video all over social media. Christina told her parents that she didn't know how he knew and exploited insecurities she had not told anyone. She said, "This feels like a spiritual battle, and he's being fed information."

Dreading the day she had to take the stage, she decided to increase the frequency and the intensity of her prayer life. She kept saying that someway, somehow, Jesus would step in and help her. The Lord was whispering in her heart, "Call out to Me, and I will defend you."

The day she had to sing arrived. All of the students were in a classroom waiting to walk into the adjacent nine-hundred-seat auditorium. Christina looked around and noticed that Zach wasn't anywhere in sight. Then, realizing that she had left her phone in the classroom, she raced to get it before she took the stage. When she walked in, she saw Zach sitting all by himself in the room, just staring at the floor. The whole scene was strangely bizarre, but she certainly didn't want to say anything to him, so she grabbed her phone and quickly left the room.

Christina took the stage and sang to her entire class, minus Zach. She received superior marks for her performance and was given the lead role in the school play.

Anxious to hear how the day went, as soon as school was over, I called my friend to ask about Christina. Christina said, "I don't know why Zach stayed in the classroom. It was as if something was keeping him in his chair." God was protecting her by keeping him in that room. We both celebrated and laughed at how God delivered her in a way no one could have ever anticipated. The tide of the battle immediately began to turn when she started to pray.

When we invite God to get involved, we witness His power. Jesus says, "*I will not leave you as orphans; **I will come to you**"* (John 14:18 ESV). King David put it this way:

> ***I prayed to the LORD, and he answered me****. He freed me from all my fears. Those who look to him for help will be radiant with joy; no shadow of shame will darken their faces.*   (Psalm 34:4–5)

I've always preferred visiting beaches over places where snow is falling. Hearing the crunch of powder-like sand under my feet never gets old. There are not many things in the world more relaxing than sitting in a chair as its legs slowly sink into the sand. If I sit soaking up the sun from the afternoon till sunset, without noticing, the waves that were once soaking my feet recede thirty feet or more. It takes six hours and twelve and a half minutes for the water at the shore to go from high tide to low tide or vice versa.[3]

QUICKER THAN THE EYE CAN OBSERVE, GOD TELLS THE WAVES WHERE TO STOP EVERY MORNING AND EVENING. IN THE SAME WAY, YOU MAY NOT SEE HOW GOD IS MOVING THE VERY DAY YOU CALL FOR HELP, BUT YOU CAN BE SURE HE IS INDEED MOVING ON YOUR BEHALF.

---

3. "Tides and Water Levels, Frequency of Tides - The Lunar Day," National Ocean Service, oceanservice.noaa.gov/education/tutorial_tides/tides05_lunarday.html.

JUST FOR YOU...

We all have one thing in common: we all need a miracle. The miracle you need may look different than mine, but we're both looking to God. It often appears as though there's no way to escape the battle we're in; we think it's our lot in life. Our vision for the future gives us strength in the present.

Do you have a dream you are about to give up on? Don't. Your dream is your fuel to carry on. The dreams you have tucked away in your heart are not selfish. They've been placed there by God.

Troubles challenge hope. Personal burdens are like a little rock in your shoe that makes every step difficult. If you can't stop to take off your shoe, sometimes you can maneuver that rock to the space in front of your toes to give you momentary comfort. In time, however, the rock creeps back under your foot, returning the ache and pain. The father of lies will tell you to stop praying and stop believing anything will ever change. Your finances will always be tight. More money will go out the door than is coming in. Your health will never improve. The rift between your close friends and those you love will never go away.

Scripture has recorded a message for you:

But when you pray, go into your room, close the door and pray to your Father, who is unseen. Then your Father, who sees what is done in secret, will reward you.

(Matthew 6:6 NIV)

Your reward isn't something you could live without. God does an inventory of your life, and He blesses you in the exact places you need it most. He doesn't give health to the healthy or give peace to those who've already received peace. He knows exactly what you need to be an overcomer. He knows how He has to move in order for the battles you face to cease.

There is no situation He cannot change. There is no heart He cannot soften. There is no person He cannot save. There is no door He cannot open. He can make the crooked places straight and the rough places smooth. He can cause everyone who sees you to like you and look at you favorably. Your Savior, Jesus Christ, can not only save your soul but also save you from any situation you're facing. You serve an almighty God!

Your God is the one who brings new relationships into your life that offer new opportunities for advancement. He is the one who can shift the variables in your life to change your entire trajectory. In an instant, He can cause the right people to look at you with favor. Over the course of your life, you can vividly remember how God moved people who tolerated you and replaced them with people who celebrate you. It's as easy for Him to change the tide of your life as it is for you to breathe.

Additionally, I would say that your dreams for yourself are smaller than God's dreams for you. If you're able to imagine the future you want, it's too small. *"Now to him who is able to do immeasurably more than all we ask or imagine, according to his power that is at work within us"* (Ephesians 3:20 NIV).

Whenever you suspect the enemy is challenging you, say, "Devil, you're a liar. I am a child of the Most High. Leave me now in the name of Jesus."

Further, I challenge you to take another bold step by praying aloud daily: "Father, I know that the very day I call for help, the tide of my battle will turn. I'm calling on You now.

You're a faithful God. I thank You ahead of time for showing Your power in my life."

PRAYER GIVES YOU THE ABILITY TO MAKE AN IMPACT

*Those who remain in me, and I in them,
will produce much fruit.*
—John 15:5

Jesus was acting differently. He was distant. He was quiet. His agony and distress were rapidly rising. He was twenty-four hours away from the cross. He wanted to escape, run into a garden, fall on His knees before His Father, and soak the ground with tears. That time would come, but not yet. He had to ensure that the message of salvation, the reason He was going to shed His blood, would be shared from generation to generation for centuries until His return.

This enormous responsibility was in the hands of a few scrappy disciples. Their commission was to a life of suffering. Ten of the twelve would ultimately face a martyr's death. As for the remaining two, Judas ended his life by hanging himself (see Matthew 27:3–10), while early Christian author Tertullian says John escaped unscathed from a vat of boiling oil before being exiled to Patmos[4] and later died of old age.

Jesus knew if His disciples were to secure the gospel, they would have to stare down fear.

To impart the strength required, Jesus needed to share one more lesson. As usual, He would use an illustration to sear the truth into their hearts. He told them, *"I am the vine; you are the branches. Those who remain in me, and I in them, will produce much fruit. For apart from me you can do nothing"* (John 15:5). Jesus wanted His disciples to see Him as a vine and themselves as His branches. A vine has a root system that goes into the ground approximately sixteen feet and can go much deeper if needed. The vine provides all the minerals required for the branch to produce fruit. Jesus was pressing

---

4. Tertullian, *The Prescription Against Heretics*, www.tertullian.org/articles/bindley_test/bindley_test_07prae.htm.

the point that those who make the daily, conscious decision to remain close to Him will produce fruit, leading to a life of immeasurable impact.

In the simplest terms, fruit is words, attitudes, or actions that bring glory to God. If we are to produce fruit that will outlast our life, the Holy Spirit must give us the ability to make lasting impressions that can forever change hearts and minds. Such a life-changing impression can only happen when God's power flows through us.

All of us are uniquely made. God has given everyone diverse spiritual gifts to display His power through us. Scripture reads, *"God has given each of you a gift from his great variety of spiritual gifts. Use them well to serve one another"* (1 Peter 4:10). As God's power flows through us, we can make an impression on people's hearts with minimal effort. A minor action or a simple sentence is filled with such force that it leads to miracles, healing, and deliverance in a single moment.

The late, great evangelist Billy Graham was among the most influential Christian leaders of the twentieth century. During his crusades, more than 2.2 million people responded to his invitation to accept Jesus Christ as their personal Savior.[5] I watched him on television preaching to tens of thousands in stadiums. I was always astounded by how the invitation was

---

5. "Billy Graham's Life & Ministry By the Numbers," Lifeway Research, February 21, 2018, research.lifeway.com/2018/02/21/billy-grahams-life-ministry-by-the-numbers.

plain and basic, yet masses of people got out of their seats and walked toward the stage to dedicate their life to Jesus. It wasn't the eloquence of the message that persuaded the crowd. The power of God flowing through Graham confirmed within them that what they were hearing was true.

I have a friend named Johnny who had the privilege of visiting with Graham in his home in North Carolina before his death. During their visit, Johnny and those with him requested prayer. Graham started his prayer by saying, "Holy Spirit, we welcome you into this room." Johnny recalls, "Immediately, the entire atmosphere of the room changed. I could truly feel the love of God. We all began to cry." Graham learned to remain closely connected to Christ Jesus, so as soon as he started praying, the Holy Spirit made Himself known. It made a lasting impression on my friend Johnny. His life will never be the same.

Sometimes, just a few words from us are all it takes to turn someone's life around. While I was on a mission trip to Bogota, Columbia, our team sat in our hotel lobby eating crackers and cheese after a long, exhausting day. One of the gentlemen on our team mentioned that he and his wife had adopted a young girl when they took a ministry trip to Bogota nearly ten years ago. He invited her to meet us, and she showed up with her friend. All was fine, but she wanted to make it clear that she was Catholic. After a series of questions, it was apparent that she had taken Jesus's mother Mary and turned her into an almost Christlike entity in the faith. Typically, convincing someone that they shouldn't be praying to Mary is a very complex conversation.

I said, "I look forward to meeting Mary when I get to heaven. I want to express my sincere appreciation for her faithfulness and obedience. However, Jesus is the one who died for your sins. Jesus is the one who rose from the grave. Therefore, He is the only one you should worship." She dropped her head, and tears flowed down her face. She devoted the rest of her life to Jesus Christ in less than a minute. This is the power of being connected to the Vine to make a lasting impression with minimal effort. All these things only happen when we choose to remain in Christ.

As Jesus continued to unpack the parable of the vine, He didn't just say that we are able to produce fruit; He said that we'll be able to produce "much fruit." Every year, our relationship will become more intimate, and the impression we're making on others will be easier and quicker.

A life producing much fruit hinges on continuous prayer. Remaining in a constant state of prayer begins with the awareness that the presence of God is all around you. Brother Lawrence said that to practice the presence of God, "we ought to act with GOD in the greatest simplicity, speaking to Him frankly and plainly, and imploring His assistance in our affairs, just as they happen."[6] Smith Wigglesworth makes such a lifestyle reachable by saying, "I don't often spend more than half

---

6. Brother Lawrence, *The Practice of the Presence of God* (London: H. R. Allenson, 1906).

an hour in prayer at one time, but I never go more than half an hour without praying."[7]

Occasionally, I travel to minister in different cities or countries. Leaving my family for a few days is not nearly as difficult as traveling to another country for a week or longer. My wife and I have a phrase we say to each other just before I leave: "Let's stay close." We promise to stay connected while I am away. We call each other, and we send messages to each other. We do all we can to ensure that we remain close.

As you are abiding in the presence of the Lord, you will notice that the Holy Spirit will softly nudge you in the direction that pleases God. He will lead you away from bitterness, rage, anger, harsh words, slander, and all types of evil behavior. The Holy Spirit will help you identify when lust and deception tempt you. Your prayers strengthen to make the decisions necessary to remain intimately connected.

When Jesus was baptized by John the Baptist, God the Father signified that He was abiding within the Father by His Spirit descending on Him like a dove. (See Luke 3:21–22.) I've heard it said that if a dove were to rest on your shoulder, and you wanted to walk without it flying away, you would need to keep that dove in mind with every step you took. Prayer and obedience keep the dove, the Holy Spirit, intimately close.

---

7. Albert Hibbert, *Smith Wigglesworth: The Secret of His Power* (Tulsa, OK: Harrison House, 1984), 47.

I'm confident that the disciples readily embraced Jesus's lesson about the vine and the branches. But I believe that within one sentence, their bright eyes dimmed. The tone changed when Jesus said that those who set their aim to produce fruit would have to learn to endure pruning. Jesus said His Father, the gardener, *"prunes the branches that do bear fruit so they will produce even more"* (John 15:2).

They knew what pruning meant; they knew their glaring weaknesses and lack of strength. They knew it could involve deep hurt. Pruning is the process of cutting or separating something from your life; it could be the loss of a relationship, income, or confidence—the list is endless. Pruning season can be one of confusion and discouragement.

But casualties can be avoided when pruning seasons are properly interpreted. These gut-wrenching seasons are not happening because you've done something wrong but because you are doing something right. Cutting away is not meant to break you. It's intended to set you in a position to produce even more fruit. When a rosebush is flush with blooming flowers, it's time for branches to be cut off. The grower knows that this process will make the bush even stronger and all the more beautiful.

I was a youth pastor in my early twenties and had momentum on my side. Attendance was growing, and we were building a dream team of adult leaders. We were developing discipleship, and most importantly, teenagers would gather at the conclusion of our services each week to dedicate their lives to Jesus Christ.

Unexpectantly, I had an opportunity to sit down with someone I greatly admired. Over lunch, he took his glasses off and laid them upside down on the table. He looked at me and said, "Frankie, you have an incredible gift to speak, but I don't believe you're called to be a pastor." His words pierced my heart all the way through. I just looked at him. I didn't know what to say. I wanted to drop my head, cover my face with my hands, and sob. My dad was a pastor, and all I ever wanted to be was a pastor. As a child, I'd preach to my teddy bears in my room and baptize my little brother in the bathtub. Now, a man whose words carried great influence in my life was telling me that I was not who I thought I was. As a result, for months I believed I should find a way to gracefully bow out and step out of ministry forever.

Faith in myself and what I've always believed my calling to be was cut out of my heart. It took many pointed conversations with my father to convince me that, although the man I admired was God-fearing, he made a massive mistake and spoke a lie into my spirit. As painful as that season was and as long-lasting as the repercussions were, with every fiber in my body, I know that if the man I admired had not hurt me in that way, I would not be as fulfilled in pastoring the church as I am today. I'm not sure what happened to me when he pruned me with his words, but years later, I know I'm stronger than

I would be otherwise. Pruning leads to greater faith, greater responsibility, and greater authority.

Peter was one of the disciples listening closely to Jesus, sharing the application of how branches that produce the most fruit are the ones that remain connected to the vine. This lesson caused him to remain tightly connected to Jesus as he endured imprisonment, persecution, and constant criticism. Many people would have crawled away into the silent shadows, but not Peter. Though he made many mistakes along the way, regardless of how much loss and devastation he faced, Peter committed his life to remaining close to Christ. As a result, the Lord allowed even those who were within Peter's shadow to be healed. (See Acts 5:15.) Every season prepares you for the next season.

JUST FOR YOU...

Since childhood, you have undoubtedly known that you were made with unique characteristics. You dreamed of all the possibilities that lay ahead. Each age of transition promises to launch you into a new season of joy. A ten-year-old longs to hit that magic number of thirteen to be a teenager. At sixteen, you can drive. At eighteen, you can finish high school and be all you know you can be. And then the storms come. Your parents are no longer able to shield you. It's time to fight for hope and dream all on your own.

Our human tendency is to look back at every moment of weakness, to wonder what life would be like if we had made different decisions. Some of those pruning seasons nearly broke you, but they didn't. Anyone else may have crumbled and failed to find the strength to stand back up and push forward. You're moving forward. You grit your teeth to endure the pruning seasons. You have refused to let go of your faith. You're committed to being an overcomer to live a life of fruitfulness. You've proven you can look up when you have no hope. This book compels you because, deep within, you know there is power in your prayers.

The interesting thing about spiritual fruit is that we always think we're producing less than we are. I promise that more people admire you than you realize. Though the people you have impacted over the years may not have told you what you've meant to them, the Lord will be pleased to show you when you get to heaven.

I encourage you to carry on. Today is the first day of the rest of your life. Imagine who you long to be and do what that person would do. Practice the presence of God. Call on the Holy Spirit to give you grace in your time of need. On the day you walk on the streets of gold, through the great pillars made of precious gems, you will be celebrated by angels.

3

PRAYER RELEASES ANGELS TO FIGHT FOR YOU

The angel of the LORD encamps around those who fear him, and he delivers them.
—Psalm 34:7 (NIV)

The angels watched with awe as God took great care and created Adam from the dust of the ground and breathed life into his nostrils. The angels were amazed when God put Adam into a deep sleep and created Eve from one of Adam's ribs.

> Then God said, "Let us make human beings in our image, to be like us." (Genesis 1:26)

The angels were captivated as they observed how God gave humans the ability to communicate, engage in complex reasoning, experience emotions, and worship. They had the ability to start families, reproduce by having children, and become fathers and mothers.

Unlike anything else God created, humans could be the Lord's companions. To the angels' amazement, God designed man and woman to live for eternity. No wonder all spiritual beings are fascinated by humankind! We rarely see angels, but they are always watching us.

CELESTIAL LIGHT BEARERS ARE COMMISSIONED TO STAND ON GUARD, DEFENDING US WHEN DEVILS COME OUR WAY. OUR GUARDIANS DO NOT COME AND GO AS VISITORS. THEY REMAIN WITH US WHETHER WE'RE SLEEPING OR AWAKE. WE ARE NEVER ALONE.

The love God has for his children reaches beyond emotion. God Almighty protects us closer than a mother over her infant baby. Like a ring of fire, the angel of the Lord encamps around us. (See Psalm 34:7.) The Lord's tenderness carefully holds our breath in His hand and triggers our hearts to beat.

This covering is reserved only for those who fear Him. The fear of the Lord is not to be frightened by His power but to be in awe of His glory. To fear the Lord is not to be afraid of Him; it's to be afraid to live without Him. The wonders of God's omnipotence compel us to lift our hands in adoration and worship Him. His love and mercy persuade us to sacrifice all selfish desires so that our only aim is to seek His face and share His love and power.

Allie and I have three children. The oldest is our daughter Preslee, then Luke, followed by Kate. One day, each of our daughters will come home with a young man who wants to ask for her hand in marriage. Naturally, I want our daughters to get married, have children, and have a beautiful family and to live a long, healthy, happy life.

Aside from deciding to dedicate their lives to Jesus, deciding who to marry is the most critical decision of our kids' lives. Therefore, I plan to have a pointed conversation with each young man before charging him with the responsibility to love and provide for our daughters, just as I have.

I will ask, "When the storm comes, and it will come, where will you run?" There is only one correct answer. I need to hear him say, in his own words, "I'll run to my Savior, my deliverer, the only one who can rescue me."

I plan to have the same conversation with my son. I know how he's been raised, and I believe in him. Even still, I'll ask him the same question. I also need to hear him say where he'll run during the storm before he's ready to provide for his wife and family. Those who lead must lead in fear of the Lord.

> THE LORD WILL NOT KEEP SORROWS, TROUBLES, AND BURDENS AWAY, BUT HE PLEDGES TO DELIVER US FROM THEM. THE SPIRIT OF THE LORD IS NOT ONLY A REFUGE; HE IS YOUR REFUGE. HE IS YOUR FORTRESS. HE IS YOUR DELIVERER.

We are pressed on every side by troubles, but we are not crushed. We are perplexed, but not driven to despair. We are hunted down, but never abandoned by God. We get knocked down, but we are not destroyed.

(2 Corinthians 4:8–9)

King Hezekiah sought God for deliverance. King Sennacherib of Assyria attacked and conquered the towns of Judah, and he sent word through his chief of staff to Hezekiah: *"What are you trusting in that makes you so confident? Do you think that mere words can substitute for military skill and strength? Who are you counting on, that you have rebelled against me?* (2 Kings 18:19–20).

The taunting message questioned Hezekiah, the people of Judah, and God. The Assyrian king's chief of staff asked Hezekiah's trusted officials if Hezekiah genuinely believed his tiny army could defeat them. He also spoke loudly enough so that the people of Judah could hear the demoralizing message. *"Don't let Hezekiah deceive you. He will never be able to rescue you. Don't let him fool you into trusting the LORD by saying, 'The LORD will surely rescue us.'"* (2 Kings 18:29–30).

"What are you trusting in?" and "Who are you counting on?" are vital questions for us today, just as they were for the Judeans. Who we trust determines the course of our life. We have all trusted friends to one degree or another. Some friends have blatantly betrayed us. Others, though with good intentions, did not have the capability of helping us. It's man's downfall to trust in man to overcome life's great struggles. For some, the all-important question of where we should put our trust has never crossed their mind.

I look up to the mountains—does my help come from there? My help comes from the LORD, who made heaven and earth!   (Psalm 121:1–2)

The blasphemous taunts and threats from the Assyrians went unanswered by Hezekiah and his people. It's better to stay quiet when you are depending on your strength. Speaking while angry and terrified is a sure way to store up regret.

Hezekiah and his officials were in such despair they tore their clothes. Horrible doubts, fears, and terrors of the grave threatened to overtake Hezekiah's hope for deliverance. All eyes pierced his heart as they looked to him for protection.

Hezekiah had his trusted officials deliver a message to the prophet Isaiah: *"Today is a day of trouble, insults, and disgrace. … But perhaps the LORD your God has heard the Assyrian chief of staff, sent by the king to defy the living God, and will punish him for his words"* (2 Kings 19:3–4). The Lord's message to Hezekiah was to not be disturbed by the Assyrian king's messengers. The Lord would move against the king.

Before engaging in battle with the king of Ethiopia, the Assyrian chief of staff met with the king of Assyria to launch another round of blasphemous insults toward God and King Hezekiah. Upon receiving the message from the Assyrians, Hezekiah went to the temple to pray to the Lord for deliverance and rescue.

As a pastor, I have seen many people who regularly attend church disappear. Months later, they'll return and tell me they've been away because they've been going through all kinds of trouble. Then they'll let me know that, now that they're back on their feet, I can expect to see them back in church. My heart breaks each time I hear this story. I think, "While you were going through such turmoil, more than ever before, you needed to be in the house of God." Hezekiah is our example of what we should do the moment life's situations turn most dire. He went to the temple.

> EVERYTHING DEPENDS ON WHO OR WHAT WE DEPEND ON. THE BATTLE OF ADDICTION CAN BREAK US DOWN. ANGER GIVES A FOOTHOLD TO THE ENEMY. HARSH WORDS CREATE ABUSIVE WORLDS. LUST OF THE FLESH MAKES PRISONERS. WE'RE WRESTLING AGAINST EVIL SPIRITS AND AUTHORITIES; WE ARE NOT WRESTLING AGAINST A PHYSICAL ENEMY, BUT A SPIRITUAL ONE.

The prophet Isaiah prayed and inquired of the Lord. He sent the message to Hezekiah that the Lord promised that the Assyrian armies would not overtake Judah. They would not even have to shoot an arrow. (See 2 Kings 19:32.) That night the angel of the Lord went out to the Assyrian camp and killed 185,000 Assyrian soldiers. When the surviving Assyrians woke up early the next morning, they found corpses everywhere. (See 2 Kings 19:35.)

Satan and his demons are the sources of all trouble. Their crafty, subtle attacks can be devastating. He whispers lies to us about who we are and who God is. His thoughts toward us are disguised as our own. We trust what we say about ourselves, so if the devil can influence our thoughts, we'll believe it's true. Despite how loud the evil beast may roar, prayer can break its teeth.

The angel of the Lord also demonstrated God's strength as Peter was shackled in chains. King Herod was on a rampage of persecuting those who called Christ their King, Savior, and Messiah. He proceeded to arrest, imprisoning him and placing him under the guard of four squads of four soldiers each. Peter was chained to the prison floor until the day he was to face a public trial.

A little group of believers gathered in a home to pray. At least one courageous believer must always speak up and say, "Let us pray." Leonard Ravenhill once said, "We need knights of prayer to lead nights of prayer."[8] They did not gather to hear a sermon or play instruments to accompany their praise. We must assemble for this reason, but the believers dedicated this

---

8. Leonard Ravenhill, *Why Revival Tarries* (Bloomington, MN: Bethany House Publishers, 2010).

time to prayer. They did not offer casual, passionless petitions. *"But while Peter was in prison, the church prayed very earnestly for him"* (Acts 12:5). There was a war in the heavens taking place, but prayer would ensure angelic intervention that would bring certain victory. May each of our homes be a house of prayer.

The prayer meeting was in Mary's house. As they prayed, an angel of the Lord appeared, and a bright light lit the cell. He bumped Peter on the side and woke him up. The chains fell off Peter's wrists, and he followed the angel out of prison. Straight away, he headed to Mary's house. The prayer meeting paused to answer the knock at the door. When they saw Peter, they were astonished! Why were they shocked? Maybe they had very little faith that God would answer their prayers. It's enlightening to discover that God honors our prayers even when we have little faith yet pray with all the faith we have.

Another possible reason for their amazement was because of how their prayers were answered. Peter was delivered that night as he was sleeping between two soldiers. It would have been a shorter reach to believe that he would receive mercy and be released during the trial. Regardless of why they were amazed, the narrative is linked to the verse that reads, *"O Israel, keep hoping, keep trusting, and keep waiting on the* Lord, *for he is tenderhearted, kind, and forgiving. He has a thousand ways to set you free"* (Psalm 130:7 TPT).

Psalm 130 is a theme verse in my life. The meaning of the number one thousand represents a concept too wonderful to comprehend. Second Peter 3:8 says, *"One day is with the Lord as a thousand years, and a thousand years as one day"* (2 Peter 3:8 kjv). The Lord is not held or constrained by time or space, and neither are His blessings and miracles.

The angel of the Lord takes great joy in surrounding, delivering, and covering us with peace that exceeds anything we can understand. He delights in sending us surprises as astonishing as that received by the small group who gave their night up in prayer. Prayer meetings are bonfires that ignite miracles. Let us multiply our requests and increase our fervor as we present our petitions and offer our worship to the Lord. One might estimate the world's weight, determine the distance to Mars, and gauge the speed of lightning, but one cannot measure the power of prayer.

JUST FOR YOU...

How many times has the Lord delivered you?

Do you remember when the Lord removed hurtful people from your life?

Do you recall the seasons when you had less than what you have now?

Look back on the season you believed you'd never get through.

You have a list of testimonies of how there was no way forward unless God stepped in, and He did. You know what rough patches feel like and how the Lord lifted you in such a way that you didn't even realize it was happening. Look where you are now. Your experiences give you influence. You have numerous stories of how the Lord delivered you from the schemes of the enemy. You can speak of how you've been set free from things that had a grip on you.

The enemy would love for you to keep your victories a secret. He'll tell you your story is no big deal, and no one cares. He knows your testimony is a weapon he cannot block. *"The testimony of Jesus is the spirit of prophecy"* (Revelation 19:10 KJV).

> ## WHEN YOU TESTIFY OF WHAT JESUS HAS DONE, YOU ARE SPEAKING OF HOW HE WILL DO IT AGAIN.

Your story has the power to bring hope. Find people to talk with, and look for moments to speak of how faithful the Lord has been to you. Bring to their attention how the angel of the Lord is close to the brokenhearted and saves those who are crushed in spirit. Your words will inject courage and strength. Be bold, and share openly what the Lord has done for you privately. When people listen to you, they'll begin to believe that if Jesus did a great work in your life, He is well able to do the same in theirs. Lives will change when people hear how your life has changed.

4

PRAYER CLOSES THE JAWS OF LIONS

My God sent his angel to shut the lions' mouths so that
they would not hurt me.
—Daniel 6:22

King Nebuchadnezzar of Babylon besieged the city of Jerusalem, taking some sacred objects from the temple of God along with captives from Judah's royal family and other noble families. These captives were loaded into long caravans, and among them was a young teenager named Daniel. The captives were young men who were strong, healthy, good-looking, well versed in every kind of learning, and of good judgment, and they were to be trained in the ways of the Babylonians.

Daniel was educated in "astronomy, astrology, divination, and the revelations of the instincts of the animal world."[9] He proved to be one of the wisest among his peers. *"God gave Daniel the special ability to interpret the meanings of visions and dreams"* (Daniel 1:17). Daniel's interpretation of King Nebuchadnezzar's dream resulted in Daniel being appointed to a high position, receiving many valuable gifts, ruling over a whole Babylonian province, and becoming chief over the king's wise men.

After Nebuchadnezzar's reign, his son Belshazzar took the throne but kept Daniel by his side. King Darius overthrew Belshazzar, but he also looked at Daniel with great favor—so much so that he planned to set him over the entire kingdom. (See Daniel 6:3). Before God would allow Daniel to receive a greater measure of authority, He had to test him.

The Lord always sends a test before a promotion. *"The LORD trieth the righteous"* (Psalm 11:5 KJV). These moments are always gut-wrenching; they feel like there is no end in sight and hope is slipping away. Hope fades when we imagine

9. Hezekiah Butterworth, "The Education of the Young Prophet Daniel," *The Biblical World* 10, no. 6 (Dec 1897): 444–53, https://www.journals. uchicago.edu/doi/pdf/10.1086/472179.

a future without the favor of God. Times of distress make us feel like some sort of loss is inevitable. The most challenging part is that a teacher rarely speaks while you're taking a test. The Lord is testing your mettle to be sure that when He blesses you with more influence, your faith is strong enough to carry the responsibility.

> *To have faith is to be sure of the things we hope for, to be certain of the things we cannot see.* (Hebrews 11:1 GNT)

If you knew what was happening to you was only a test, you would certainly have the strength to carry on. Therefore, children of God must learn to whisper to themselves, "This is only a test." When someone provokes you, just say, "This is only a test." When anger begins to boil, just say, "This is only a test." When temptation rushes in, just say, "This is only a test."

King Darius signed into law a devious plan put forth by his administrators and high officers designed to test Daniel's faithfulness to the king. *"Give orders that for the next thirty days any person who prays to anyone, divine or human—except to you, Your Majesty—will be thrown into the den of lions"* (Daniel 6:7).

The only way to stand in the midst of trouble is to remain kneeling before God. Prayer gives us the power to carry on and the grace to bounce back from our moments of weakness. Despite the new decree, Daniel continued to pray to the Lord three times a day with his windows open in the second-floor room of his home. King Darius's officials found Daniel in prayer and informed the king. The king could not go back on his law no matter how much he respected Daniel. Consequently, Daniel was immediately arrested and was sentenced to be thrown into the den of lions.

> ## OUR FAITH GROWS AS WE WITNESS HOW GOD INTERVENES DURING TIMES OF TROUBLE.

Daniel had to face the demonic lions before he met the den of lions. The voices of devils are internal. They disguise their voices to sound like our own thoughts. Their words are so subtle you can hardly notice they're spoken by a devil. "Daniel, you've gone too far this time. You could have easily prayed in private and avoided a death sentence. You're going to be torn apart!"

We have no ability to mute spirits. The only way to conquer an evil spirit is to call on the Holy Spirit. We are victorious when our prayers echo David's words, *"In your unfailing love, silence my enemies; destroy all my foes, for I am your servant"* (Psalm 143:12 NIV).

King Darius was greatly distressed about having to punish Daniel. He said, *"May your God, whom you serve continually, deliver you!"* (Daniel 6:16 ESV). Daniel wasn't escorted through a gate to be fed to the wild beasts. He was thrown down a funnel-shaped cistern dug out of the ground that had a small opening that would have been covered with a stone.[10] The sheer impact of the fall could have easily injured him. The roar of the lions, which can be heard up to five miles away, was deafening. The jaws of the lions were wide open, showing their three-inch canine fangs. Surely the sight would have shaken every bone in Daniel's body. God was testing Daniel. Satan was witnessing. People all around were watching. Everyone wants to know if children of God can continue to worship in a den of lions. It's easy to worship in the sanctuary, but can we worship in the den?

At the first light of dawn, King Darius got up and ran to the den and called to Daniel in an anguished voice, *"Daniel, servant of the living God, has your God, who you serve continually, been able to rescue you from the lions?"* (Daniel 6:20 NIV). King Darius knew Daniel could only survive the night if his God saved him. What shock and joy he must have felt when he heard Daniel lift his voice in praise and say, *"God sent his angel, and he shut the mouths of the lions. They have not hurt me"* (Daniel 6:22 NIV). Lions lying closely against Daniel like pets must be one of the most extraordinary scenes in history.

Everyone's faith will be tested at one time or another. The rain will fall, the floods will come, the winds will blow,

10. Karl Keil and Franz Delitzsch, "Keil and Delitzsch OT Commentary: Daniel 6," Bible Hub, September 22, 2023, https://biblehub.com/commentaries/kad/daniel/6.htm.

and every house will reveal whether it is built on sand or on the rock. (See Matthew 7:24–26.) We demonstrate our faith during storms. Our testimony of God's faithfulness makes its greatest impact in moments when we need a great miracle.

If Daniel had given in to the temptation to close his mouth, he would have been giving up the separated life. He knew that he could not make a difference in this world if there were no difference between him and the world. Acting as others act is the temptation all will face. It's the fear of lions mocking us that we want to avoid. Often, we're tempted not to speak of our Lord because we know that if we're ever weak, the lions around us will laugh and jeer. The enemy makes us believe that simple confessions such as, "My God is perfect. I'm not. His love and mercy upon me are why I worship Him" will not be enough. Remember that people will respect you because of your strengths but connect to you because of your weaknesses.

> TODAY'S LIONS ARE NOT ANIMALS; THEY'RE EVIL SPIRITS THAT AIM TO CONDEMN YOU AND PEOPLE WHO THREATEN YOU. JUST LIKE GOD RESCUED DANIEL, HE WILL SEND ANGELS TO CLOSE THE JAWS OF YOUR ENEMIES.

I led a very sinful life during my years in high school in Houston, Texas, and continued into my freshman year of college. I had a transformative life experience when I met lead pastors from a church in Rockford, Illinois. They invited me to move into their city to be a part of a ministerial intern program while attending Bible college. My passion for Christ overtook my entire life. I met Allie, the girl of my dreams, and proposed in a carriage pulled by two white horses on the snowy streets of Chicago. We were so happy living in Illinois—we never intended to leave. We wanted to raise our family in the same city that brought us together.

A pastor in the Houston area called my pastor to ask if they knew of anyone who would be a good fit for them to hire as their youth director. Since I was from Houston, they referred Allie and me. Immediately, I said absolutely not. I had done too many things in Houston, and I didn't want to live in fear that someone from high school would track me down and shout out everything I wished I had never done.

Through a series of events, the Lord made it clear that He wanted my wife and I to move to Houston and accept the position. For years I worried that someone from my past would show up and criticize me, but it never happened. Decades went by, and not one person showed up to tell stories of what I was like before the Lord rescued me. The Lord had not only forgiven me for my past but had also silenced my accusers.

Lions are kittens in the eyes of God. Your present and your future are delicately held in the hand of God. He is always for you. Even when you have made foolish decisions that caused collateral damage, God is always at work, arranging for setbacks to give you more experience, wisdom, and strength as He guides you into your next assignment. The plans He has for you are not contingent upon you remaining strong at all times.

Our Father in heaven remembers how you were formed. He knows you were made from dust. He will not reject a broken and repentant heart; He will always raise up the humble. As you walk through heaven's gates, you will be celebrated for your endurance, tenacity, and the significant contributions you've made for the kingdom of God. You're a child of the King. You're destined to be an inspiration that will have the power to shift the flight paths of lives all around you.

Your enemy, who's always on the attack, is afraid of you. He knows that if he cannot keep you from praying, the arrows of worry will have no effect on you.

Earl Nightingale wrote an article about worry and anxiety I believe will significantly encourage you.

THE FOG OF WORRY
(ONLY 8% OF WORRIES ARE WORTH IT)

According to the Bureau of Standards, "A dense fog covering seven city blocks, to a depth of 100 feet, is composed of something less than one glass of water." So, if all the fog covering seven city blocks, 100 feet deep, were collected and held in a single drinking glass, it would not even fill it. And this could be compared to our worries. If we can see into the future and if we could see our problems in their true light, they wouldn't tend to blind us to the world, to living itself, but instead could be relegated to their true size and place. And if all the things most people worry about were reduced to their true size, you could probably put them all into a drinking glass, too.

It's a well-established fact that as we get older, we worry less. With the passing of the years and the problems each of them yields, we learn that most of our worries are not really worth bothering ourselves about too much and that we can manage to solve the important ones.

But to younger people, they often find their lives obscured by the fog of worry. Yet, here's an authoritative estimate of what most people worry about.

1. Things that never happen: 40 percent. That is, 40 percent of the things you worry about will never occur anyway.

2. Things over and past that can't be changed by all the worry in the world: 30 percent.

3. Needless worries about our health: 12 percent.

4. Petty, miscellaneous worries: 10 percent.

5. Real, legitimate worries: 8 percent. Only 8 percent of your worries are worth concerning yourself about. Ninety-two percent are pure fog with no substance at all.[11]

---

11. Earl Nightingale, "The Fog of Worry: Only 8 of Worries Are Worth It," https://www.nightingale.com/articles/the-fog-of-worry-only-8-of-worries-are-worth-it/.

JUST FOR YOU...

If you ever hear the roar of a lion breathing threats as you're placing your trust in God's victorious right hand, remind yourself that this is only a test. Know that small steps in the right direction are big steps away from the wrong direction. Lastly, and most importantly, ask the Holy Spirit to help you ensure that not an hour goes past without you praying. Your prayers are what compels God to send angels to shut the mouths of lions.

5

PRAYER IGNITES A THOUSAND WAYS GOD SETS YOU FREE

*O Israel, keep hoping, keep trusting, and keep waiting
on the LORD, for he is tenderhearted, kind, and forgiving. He has a thousand ways to set you free!*
—Psalm 130:7 (TPT).

The psalmist was confessing his sins and begging for forgive-
ness when he wrote chapter 130 in the book of Psalms. His

sins were ever before him. He couldn't stop thinking about the consequences of his actions. He believed he had jeopardized the favor of God in his life; his fate was doomed, and there was nothing he could do about it. Every good thing in his life was sure to be stripped away. He was sure his family would abandon him and his friends would turn their backs. It's common to forget how much we love our family, and we take good health for granted. I once heard a doctor say that we never think about our heart, nor do we notice it, until it skips a beat.

The psalmist wrote Psalm 130 to describe how he was delivered, how his sins were pardoned, and how he was rescued from life's most extreme distress. He chronicled how God's mercy is unfailing in order to encourage you and I that God has no favorites, so He will also save all wrestling believers from similar, overwhelming circumstances. The psalmist was not unfamiliar with feeling abandoned, hurt, or shame. If he were, he would not have been able to earn our trust. Psalm 130 is a reminder that the psalmist walked the same road as all of us. He lived on to tell of how the presence of the Lord rushed to him and gave him unmerited comfort.

"Keep hoping, keep trusting, and keep waiting on the Lord*"* (Psalm 130:7 TPT). David's words seem to urge us not to delay our call for help.

If our plan to get out of trouble is to strategize our way forward, it will take too long and be full of mistakes and missteps. If we could pull ourselves out of conflict, we would do it; the fact that we're still in it for days, weeks, months, and sometimes even longer proves we cannot rescue ourselves.

> ## WAITING IDLY FOR OUR DISTRESSES TO PASS IS NOT HOW THE SPIRIT OF THE LORD WANTS US TO LIVE.

KEEP HOPING.

These words are not for those who are tiptoeing through the tulips of life. It's for those who feel the tension between hanging on to hope and letting go.

One of the most challenging seasons in my marriage was when Allie, the love of my life, was so sick she couldn't get out of bed but for a few moments at a time. Our three children were scared their mommy would never get better. The most discouraging part was we could not find a doctor who could diagnose the issue. They were throwing darts at what could be the problem but missed every time.

Hope deferred makes the heart sick.   (Proverbs 13:12)

I noticed that the less I prayed throughout the day, the quicker despair set in. When my hope dropped, it had a direct effect on whether our children would continue to believe their mother would be healed. We often don't realize how much others are depending on our faith to strengthen their faith. If I concentrated on praying wherever I was and whatever I was doing, my expectations would rise, and I'd feel an assurance that healing was on its way.

While playing basketball at a local gym, I met a neurosurgeon. I told him about Allie, and he asked for an opportunity to meet with her. He concluded that she had a spinal leak, which was causing the frontal lobe of her brain to dry out. He gave her an epidural, and within a few weeks, she was one hundred percent better. Looking back, I'm still amazed that God arranged for me to meet the right doctor while playing basketball, of all places. The Spirit of the Lord will prove that our hope will not end in disappointment.

KEEP TRUSTING.

There is a narrative in Scripture of a woman who had an issue of blood and had been hemorrhaging for twelve years. She had spent all her money paying doctors, but each was unable to help. In fact, her condition only worsened.

One day, she encountered a crowd of people following Jesus. She had heard about His ability to deliver people from devils and to heal the sick. For the first time in over a decade, she saw a man she believed she could trust. She decided to squeeze her way through the crowd to get close to Him.

"Coming up behind Jesus, she touched the fringe of his robe. Immediately, the bleeding stopped" (Luke 8:44). If the bleeding stopped immediately, that meant she was bleeding as she pressed her way through the crowd. Having dealt with this issue for so long, she knew how much time she had before others would notice she was hemorrhaging. Being embarrassed and humiliated was a very real possibility.

DESPERATE PEOPLE DO NOT WAIT ON THE LORD; THEY PURSUE HIM.

To have faith is to wage war between trust and risk. As the woman drew closer to Jesus, she didn't want to draw attention to herself, so she bent low and touched the hem of His robe. Immediately, the bleeding stopped. Her faith should serve as an inspiration to us because she believed the words in her heart that said, "Keep on trusting."

KEEP WAITING.

The psalmist goes on to write, *"Keep waiting on the LORD, for he is tenderhearted, kind, and forgiving"* (Psalm 130:7 TPT). A tender heart feels our joy and laughs with us; it feels our pain and hurts with us. Jesus is fully aware of the difficulties, battles, and troubles that plague us. He knows we are feeble-kneed. He's aware of how our body gets weaker as we get older. He knows we struggle to keep our emotions from running out of control, and He sees the burdens we carry. Jesus assures us He understands; *"We do not have a high priest who is unable to empathize with our weaknesses"* (Hebrews 4:15 NIV). Jesus was despised and rejected, a man of sorrows and familiar with suffering. (See Isaiah 53:3.) He has compassion on us just as a father and mother have compassion on their hurting child.

"Something about her skin color doesn't look right." Those were the words of the doctor immediately after Preslee, our oldest daughter, was born. He snatched her up before her mother or I could hold her for the first time. He told the nurses to immediately take her to the intensive care unit. Her lungs weren't functioning properly, which caused her to breathe with difficulty. My heart tore as I watched her struggle. The only thing I could do was look through the window and watch her in the hands of the hospital staff. I'd report back to Allie how she was doing. Eventually, Preslee's health and strength increased, and we were able to bring her home in perfect health.

Luke, our second child, screamed for the majority of the first six months after his birth. We tried everything we could, but we could not figure out how to calm him. We'd walk him around the block, we'd buy toys that should have been interesting for children his age, but nothing worked. We took him to the doctor several times, but they offered no answers. We shifted to another doctor to get another opinion, and she discovered that he was in distress because he was having middle ear infections. We learned that these were difficult to treat with antibiotics, especially in Luke's case because he was retaining fluid in between the infections. The solution was to have ear tubes placed in his ears. Again, Allie and I experienced the kind of compassion only a mother and father can feel.

Our third child, Kate, was born with her right toes pointing toward her left foot. As she tried to walk, she'd often kick her own leg and fall to the ground. The pediatrician took a photo of her and saw that one leg was clearly significantly longer than the other. We were more than shaken, but the doctor said that as her hips widened with age, by around ten years old, all would be corrected, and her leg and foot would be completely normal. If you're a parent, you know how your heart sinks and rises according to how your children are doing.

Late one night, after our children were tucked into bed, I was walking the block crying out to the Lord to help me in my distress. The anxiety had reached a point I could no longer handle. I felt as if I were trying to talk Him into helping me. As I headed back home, a thought flashed through my mind.

At that very moment, I felt the tenderness of His heart, and it flooded me with peace. The things that concerned me took a few weeks to get ironed out, but I only felt peace from that moment forward.

> I KNEW THE LORD WAS ASKING ME,
> "DO YOU THINK YOU ARE A BETTER FATHER THAN
> ME?" THE MOMENT WAS INCREDIBLY EMOTIONAL
> AS I DIDN'T EVEN HAVE TO ANSWER HIM;
> HE KNEW I KNEW THE ANSWER.

A friend of mine was praying one morning and received the revelation that one of the reasons God gave us the ability to love our children so deeply was to give us a glimpse of how much He loves us.

The psalmist continues to share that *"God is kind and forgiving"* (Psalm 130:7 TPT). We cannot blink faster than God forgives. *"As far as the east is from the west, so far has he removed our transgressions from us"* (Psalm 103:12 NIV). Every time the devil reminds you of the sins of your past, say, "I'm not that person anymore. I've been washed by the blood of Jesus. I've been made new. Leave me now in the name of Jesus!"

At the end of the verse, the psalmist announces, *"He has a thousand ways to set you free"* (Psalm 130:7 TPT). On my best day, if I strain my imagination, I can think of two or three different ways God could relieve me from all my difficulties. I'm confident you can smile and say the same.

JUST FOR YOU...

When life gets chaotic, during the waiting, set your sights on small targets. The first target is to aim for moment-by-moment obedience. Daily you will surely need to make split-second decisions to do, think about, and say the right thing. Every small step in the right direction is a massive step from going in the wrong direction. All moments of obedience keep the enemy from gaining a foothold. You will feel the pleasure of the Lord at this moment because He notices them all.

A second target is to aim to bless the Lord continually. There is no need to scramble for eloquent words. Memorize the verse which has been the foundation of this chapter, *"O Israel, keep hoping, keep trusting, and keep waiting on the* LORD, *for he is tenderhearted, kind, and forgiving. He has a thousand ways to set you free"* (Psalm 130:7 TPT), and pray one part of the verse at a time. "Jesus, I thank You that I can put my hope and my trust in You. I thank You that You're safe enough for me to wait upon. I praise You for being tenderhearted, kind, and forgiving."

From there, continue to praise the Lord for the simple blessings we often overlook. "Jesus, thank You for my eyesight, my hearing, for muscles and strong bones. Thank You for giving me a home and a bed where I can lie down and rest. Thank You for a refrigerator full of food." As you acknowledge the basics, the Holy Spirit will remind you of the countless other reasons to praise your Savior. As you praise Him, though the world may be spinning fast, you'll find perfect peace within the three-foot circle around you.

6

PRAYER KINDLES YOUR INTIMACY WITH GOD

Our fellowship is with the Father and with his Son,
Jesus Christ.
—1 John 1:3

Jesus and John were essentially "best friends." Early church tradition unanimously identified *"the disciple whom Jesus loved"* (John 21:20) as John. John seemed to have a closer relationship with Jesus than any of the other disciples did. John laid his head upon Christ's chest (see John 13:23); he laid all his thoughts and all his emotions upon the affection of his Lord. After Christ was resurrected and returned to His Father, John no longer walked with Jesus in the flesh. He could no longer touch Him with his hands. However, John's relationship with Jesus never changed; they remained just as close as they had always been. John says, *"Our fellowship is with the Father and with his Son, Jesus Christ"* (1 John 1:3). John didn't say that his fellowship *was* with the Father and His Son Jesus; he said that it *is*. He wasn't referring to the past; he was speaking of what it was like in the present moment. Whether Jesus was sitting at a table next to John or sitting at the right hand of the Father, John's fellowship with Him was just the same.

John never stopped having conversations with God. The secret to intimacy is to pray in secret. Talking with God is to take place all day, every day. While you're alone, you can pause your day, lift your eyes toward heaven, and have an intimate moment with the Lord. It may not last but a few moments, but you know the moment was special. You're just taking a little time to say, "Yes, there is a lot I need to do today, but right now, I want You to know that You're all I truly love. You're everything to me. I will spend my life worshiping You!"

In between these pauses, the Holy Spirit will cause your thoughts to drift toward the Lord so you may send thoughts of affection in His direction. In turn, the Lord will do the same, causing your entire life to be one intimate moment after another. Anyone who has ever experienced such a relationship will protect it until their very last breath; it's the most special part of their life. All other things in this world are worthless. John writes of his relationship so all who want the same know precisely how to ignite it.

It's in the Scriptures that we discover the secrets of God. Therefore, if we genuinely want to be close to the Lord, we're going to have to create gaps of time to read the Bible. I've learned that these gaps never come without a sacrifice. In a busy world, it's rare to have moments when we can sit and read. We must make time. Living for the Lord without being familiar with Scripture leads to a misunderstood relationship.

IT'S IN GOD'S WORD THAT WE GET TO KNOW THE HEART OF GOD. WE LEARN WHO HE IS AND WHAT HE LOVES.

Those who do not read the Bible are in great danger of building their own theology. They'll start their sentences off by saying, "Well, I just believe …" rather than, "The Bible says …" Those who desire intimacy with God make time to read Scripture.

I trained for almost a year for a 70.3 Ironman. The race involves a 1.2-mile swim, 56 miles of biking, and 13.1 miles of running. I didn't have the time in the morning, afternoon, or evening to train for each of the three legs of the race. I had to make the time. The only way to make time was to wake up early. I vividly remember running down the street while the streetlights lit up the road. Before sunrise, I'd go to a gym that would open early and swim laps back and forth. Remembering this season of my life reminds me that we make time for what we find important.

I have friends whose conversations with God happen when they go to a quiet place with a journal and say, "Jesus, I want to talk with you." As they write their own prayers, they'll start writing thoughts that are directed to them. Their hand begins writing faster than they're thinking, giving them the assurance that the Spirit of the Lord is speaking. The advantage of journaling is it gives you the ability to reflect and remind yourself of all the Lord has spoken to you.

As for myself, I block off a time to be alone with God, and I begin the conversation by telling Him how much I love Him, and then I say, "Lord, I want you to speak to me." When I do this, I receive an impression, or a thought that has no relation to what I was already thinking. It's like a flash of a thought. It's at that point that the Holy Spirit and I begin to trade thoughts that go on as long as I'm willing to continue. Admittedly, there are times when I wonder if these thoughts are indeed from the Holy Spirit. I'm quickly reminded that what is happening only happens when I'm in a conversation with God. Additionally, it's in these moments that I become aware of how much the

Lord loves me. I can feel peace and assurance that He has plans for me.

The most treasured part of having intimate fellowship with the Holy Spirit is being able to, in a split second, become aware of the Spirit of the Lord's presence. Others may have to have perfect conditions in order to have this awareness, such as being in church on a Sunday morning. Those who are intimate with the Lord can have these moments any time they want. Countless times, every hour of the day, you're able to have a sense of knowing that the Holy Spirit is beside you. These moments are His way of saying, "Right now, I want you to know I'm close to you, and I love you." The more you respond by simply saying, "I love You," the more regularly these moments will occur.

Our heavenly Father is so full of kindness, He blesses people who do not even acknowledge Him. From His abundant love, there are certain blessings He gives to everyone. *"For the life of every living thing is in his hand, and the breath of every human being"* (Job 12:10). However, there are specific gifts that are reserved only for those who walk intimately with the Lord. Joy is one of those most priceless gifts.

For the majority of the world, joy is elusive. Material possessions are unable to provide us with the joy we seek. Joy does include laughter and even feelings of happiness, but its depth is far more profound. Joy slows your life down just enough for you to take pleasure in all Jesus has given you. You cherish the simplest things. All day you'll take a minute to smile and be grateful.

I first started noticing the Lord had given me joy when I found myself looking across the room, smiling at my wife and kids. Busyness no longer pulls me away from enjoying being in their company. I'm always telling them how much I love them, leaving them notes, and calling them. If I weren't closely walking with the Lord, I'd give all other cares more attention than the only ones in my life I'd lay my life down for.

My wife laughs at me every morning because she and my kids know that the first thing I'm going to do when I wake up is make a cup of coffee and walk around my backyard admiring every plant and tree I've ever planted. I'll ask my family, "Who's green grass is that?" That's their cue to say, "That's our grass!" Enjoying the littlest things in life is an indication that the Lord has given you a gift of joy.

Demons do not allow the treasure of walking with the Lord to go uncontested. Evil spirits do not sit back and freely allow us to enjoy walking "*in close fellowship with God*" (Genesis 5:22), as Enoch experienced. It's staggering how responsive devils are. They attack the very second your attention leans toward the Holy Spirit. The two things the enemy will most often use to interrupt our intimacy with God are the lure of wealth and the lust for destructive passions. Like any good fisherman, the devil always shows the bait and hides the hook. He makes us believe that there is a parallel path to our relationship with God that will bring great fulfillment and happiness. There is no parallel path. One cannot be as passionate about temporal things as they are about spiritual things. One must dominate the other.

I cannot think of anyone who has told me that they don't need any more money. I've met incredibly wealthy people who have more money than they'll ever spend and remain unsatisfied. John D. Rockefeller, an American businessman, has been widely considered the wealthiest American of all time and the richest person in modern history. At the peak of his wealth, Rockefeller had a net worth of about 1 percent of the entire US economy. He owned 90 percent of the oil and gas industry of his time. [12] When he was asked how much money is enough money, he said, "Just a little bit more."[13]

Destructive passions are like an army of little devils sent to destroy your life. These passions cause us to believe that, without them, our life would be miserable. Lust, addictions, and being entertained by sin are like sharp, jaw-like clamps that take a deathly hold on a wild beast. Everyone must choose to sacrifice lustful desires or sacrifice intimacy with the Lord. Only one must live. This world presents endless competing passions that force us to surrender the life we're tempted to live for the life God wants us to live.

---

12. Byron Moore, "How Much Money Is Enough," *Shreveport Times*, December 10, 2017, https://www.shreveporttimes.com/story/news/local/blogs/2017/12/10/how-much-money-enough/930449001/.
13. Moore, "How Much Money Is Enough."

I heard a story of a grandfather petting his cat from its tail to its head. His grandson told him that he was petting the cat backward. He replied, "Well, the cat better turn around." The grandfather was not going to change. Our Father in heaven is the same yesterday, today, and forever. The things He loves, He'll always love. The things He hates, He'll always hate.

> ## TRUE SUBMISSION CAN ONLY BE PROVEN WHEN THERE IS A CLASH BETWEEN OUR DESIRES AND GOD'S DESIRES.

One may look to a friend and say, "I've loved what the Bible calls sin as far back as I can remember. I believe I was born this way." The friend could quickly reply, "I'm not tempted by what you are, but the temptations I fight have also been with me since I was a child." Temptation may look different for everyone, but no one should believe they're the only one who has an intense battle to fight.

It's common to think that your struggles are more significant than others, but rest assured, no struggle is an easy struggle. The Spirit of the Lord anticipated we were going to have a grueling war on our hands, so He was sure to have it written, *"The righteous person faces many troubles, but the LORD comes to the rescue each time"* (Psalm 34:19). No one will ever have the strength to overcome every trap the enemy sets before us if we're depending on our own discipline. Devils laugh at our strength, but they run when we call on the power of the Lord.

As far back as I can remember, I've always wanted to be a man the Lord could use, but in order for that to ever be possible, I knew my heart and mind would have to be completely rewired. The only thing I knew to do was to pray one-sentence prayers throughout the day. Little did I realize that each sentence I prayed was building intimacy with the Holy Spirit. Short prayers are powerful prayers. I don't know how or when it happened, but the Holy Spirit began to give me a new heart and new spirit. As I started to see how sin was rampant everywhere, I felt a holy anger toward the enemy. Over time, I realized that when I spoke of the Lord, the words would often burn in people's hearts.

A scripture in the Bible gives us the secret to overcoming the sin that can easily entangle us. *"Walk in the Spirit, and you shall not fulfill the lust of the flesh"* (Galatians 5:16 NKJV). In other words, stay focused on walking with the Holy Spirit, and the result will be that you'll become stronger and stronger so that no lust will overcome you. The things that once controlled you will be a part of your testimony.

Night and day, whether you are asleep or awake, your relationship with the Lord is becoming stronger and more intimate than ever before. The closeness you'll have with the Holy Spirit will begin each morning before you open your eyes.

You'll pause your day and lift your hands and voice to worship the Lord. You will create a sanctuary wherever you go. Your thoughts will continually drift toward the Lord, and you'll recognize His thoughts toward you. This will be the story of your life.

JUST FOR YOU...

Charles Swindoll once said, "I cannot even imagine where I would be today were it not for that handful of friends who have given me a heart full of joy. Let's face it; friends make life a lot more fun."[14] If you have one good friend, you have more good friends than half the people in the world have. Even though your friends sincerely care about you, there are needs they will never meet. They'll never understand your deepest thoughts.

---

14. Charles R. Swindoll, *Laugh Again / Hope Again: Two Books to Inspire a Joy-Filled Life.* (Nashville: Thomas Nelson, 2009), 96.

The Holy Spirit's primary role in your life is to be your comforter. He longs to be your closest friend. He is the only one who knows you so intimately, He knows what you're going to say before you say it. Even still, say what you're thinking anyway. He loves the sound of your voice.

7

PRAYER PRODUCES POWER WITHIN

*Now to him who is able to do immeasurably
more than all we ask or imagine, according to his power
that is at work within us.*
—Ephesians 3:20 (NIV)

The words in today's opening verse are not journal entries. They are not written prayers. These verses are the highest praise the apostle Paul can offer to the Lord. We must make it the pattern of our lives to stop whatever we're doing to praise the Lord. I love the refrain of the old hymn that says,

> Turn your eyes upon Jesus,
>
> Look full in His wonderful face,
>
> And the things of earth will grow strangely dim,
>
> In the light of His glory and grace.[15]

Those who worship know this to be true.

The apostle's praise reads, *"Now to him who is able to do immeasurably more than all we ask or imagine, according to his power that is at work within us"* (Ephesians 3:20 NIV). The scripture emphasizes how God blesses us beyond what we are asking for. The prayer requests we've all made over the course of our life cannot be numbered. Even so, our boldest prayers are light-years away from acknowledging how capable God is of accomplishing above and beyond what we are requesting. If we're honest, from day to day, we hardly know what we really need from God. Thankfully, He isn't limited by our limited imagination. In His loving-kindness, He is uninterested in simply providing for our needs; He wants to exceed our expectations.

Technically, children do not need more than a few shirts, a couple of pairs of pants, and some shoes. Yet no parent wants

---

15. Helen H. Lemmel, "Turn Your Eyes Upon Jesus" (1922), https://hymnary.org/text/o_soul_are_you_weary_and_troubled.

to give their children the bare essentials. They want their children to have all they're able to afford. Parents feel proud when their kids look good. All the more, your Father in heaven doesn't want you to receive only the things you think you need. He desires for you to live a life overwhelmed with blessings you didn't even know to ask for.

It's the Lord's desire that we pray about all things at all times. (See 1 Thessalonians 5:17.) Additionally, we need to remember to pray for the things we cannot imagine. As we come to the Lord, let us say, "Lord, You know my requests. You're aware of my needs, but I also ask for You to give me the things my imagination cannot fathom. Overwhelm me!"

My wife and I used to live forty-five minutes outside the city where we started our church. We desired to live closer to the church, and we were able to find a small house to rent. An opportunity was soon presented to us to build our own home. We were able to pick out the bricks as well as other building materials. We'd drive by a couple of times a week just to walk through the rooms as they were being built. We were so excited at the thought of living closer to the church and living in our newly built home.

Our church did not have a building to call its own during this time. We rented an elementary school each Sunday to hold our services. We began to experience growth throughout the church, and the local high school provided a much larger space for our congregation to meet. The rent for the high school was significantly higher than the elementary school, though. For the church to afford the rent, Allie and I needed to take a cut in our salary. We were thrilled the church was growing, but we were heartbroken about having to walk away from our new house.

About six months later, I received an email from a friend who was moving to another city. He inquired if Allie and I wanted to buy his house. The house was much larger than the one we were building, and it was nestled on five acres of property. He insisted that he wanted to sell the house for a price that would allow our mortgage payments to be equal to what we were currently paying in rent. He reduced the house's sale price by 75 percent for that to happen. This home far exceeded our wildest imagination. These are the things the apostle was referring to. Our dreams are not big enough.

After a couple of years of marriage, my friend Thiago and his wife Rebeca decided to begin trying to have a baby. Despite all their efforts, they experienced one complication after another. Their doctor pleaded with them to stop trying because it could put Rebeca's health at risk. I remember the tears that filled Thiago's eyes when he shared the devastating news.

Thiago and I were at lunch one day while traveling on a ministry trip to Brazil. There were close to a dozen people at the table, half of whom we had never met before. Thiago introduced himself to John, who was sitting across from us. As they exchanged pleasantries, John said to him, "My parents thought they were not able to have children. I was a miracle baby. I believe the Lord wants me to tell you that you're going to have a miracle baby." Thiago nearly fell out of his seat. He couldn't believe what he had just heard. He returned to the hotel and called his wife to tell her what John had said. She replied, "I just took a pregnancy test. I'm pregnant!" Unbeknownst to either of them, Rebeca had been pregnant for nearly two weeks! They had a beautiful baby girl named Sophia. I believe Thiago and Rebeca went to sleep smiling every night for a month. God answered their prayer. Twelve months later, Rebeca sat down with Thiago to tell him that she was pregnant again! Now they have two baby girls, Sophia and Bella. God did immeasurably more than what they asked for.

The second half of Ephesians 3:20 is equally exciting: "*Now to him who is able to do immeasurably more than all we ask or imagine, **according to his power that is at work within us***" (Ephesians 3:20 NIV). Our bodies are marvelous master-pieces of God's creation. Our lungs inhale oxygen and exhale carbon dioxide. This process happens approximately twenty-two thousand times a day.[16] Our hearts beat approximately one hundred thousand times each day and roughly thirty-five million times in a year.[17]

---

16. Canadian Lung Association, "Breathing," The Lung Association, September 13, 2023, https://www.lung.ca/lung-health/lung-info/breathing.
17. NOVA Online. "Cut to the Heart: Amazing Heart Facts," PBS, April 8, 1997, https://www.pbs.org/wgbh/nova/heart/heartfacts.html.

As impressive as the human body may be, Paul tells us that the power of God is also at work within us. Imagine that the God who lit the sun on fire is working in us. The variety of ways God's power is manifested cannot be conceived. Such knowledge is too wonderful and too excellent to understand. (See Psalm 139:6.) What I am able to acknowledge is that God's power in us works differently from person to person.

In Acts 6:8–8:2 we learn that Stephen, "*a man full of God's grace and power, performed amazing miracles and signs among the people*" (Acts 6:8). If a person can be full of God's power, that would lead us to believe that someone could be partially full or even not full at all. Not all of Christ's followers were blessed with the amount of power Stephen was given. In the life of Stephen, we see that there are levels to miracles. Others in Scripture performed miracles, but Stephen performed "*amazing*" miracles. If we were there, I'm sure we would see the difference.

An analogy I once read can give us more insight. The human brain is a complex organ and the informational data center for our bodies. It's capable of recalling, applying, and absorbing a vast amount of knowledge. Our abilities are according to the amount of knowledge that is at work within us. It's our job to challenge ourselves to learn as much as we can and to increase our base of knowledge so that we are able to solve problems, understand the complexities of life, and possess all the understanding necessary to be successful at whatever we do. In the same way, how often we pray, how long we pray, and how passionate we are when we pray is directly linked to the amount of power that is at work within us. In turn, it determines how much God is able to do in our lives.

Men and women who testify of how God has mightily used them are not loved any more than anyone else. It's not as if they've been selected for a higher calling than everyone else. If you interview them, the only difference between their life and everyone else's is that they seek the face of God with more diligence and passion. These people shake their head in amazement because their life is full of memories of God doing more than they could have asked for. Every single prayer you pray ignites more of God's power working within you.

Supernatural acceleration is a very real thing. This is when God hears your voice and causes things that should take years to take place to happen in a fraction of the time. When we lift our voices to the Lord, a supernatural power ignites to cause acceleration.

The people of Israel had been in a continual pattern of murmuring and complaining against Moses and Aaron. The Lord instructed Moses to tell the people to bring twelve wooden staffs, one representing each leader of Israel's tribes. Each staff was to have a leader's name inscribed on it. Aaron's name was inscribed on the tribe of Levi's staff.

After the inscriptions were completed, Moses placed the staffs in the Lord's presence in the tabernacle of the covenant. The staff that began to sprout buds would signify which leader

God chose. "*When he went into the Tabernacle of the Covenant the next day, he found that Aaron's staff, representing the tribe of Levi, had sprouted, budded, blossomed, and produced ripe almonds!*" (Numbers 17:8). The riot against Moses and Aaron could have lasted for weeks, even months, but God brought resolution within twenty-four hours.

Elijah had been living in the midst of a drought for three years. There was neither dew nor rain. Crops could not grow, animals could not eat, and the people were helpless. "*Elijah climbed to the top of Carmel, bent down to the ground and put his face between his knees*" (1 Kings 18:42 NIV). Like when we drive a car with a manual transmission, there are different gears we can learn to shift into when we pray. Praying for your breakfast in the morning could be considered as first gear. The highest gear would be used when the situation is most dire. You'll cry out before the Lord for as long as it takes.

Elijah prayed for rain and instructed his servant to look toward the sea. The servant saw nothing. This happened seven times, Elijah and his servant going back and forth. The seventh time, the servant spotted and reported to Elijah that a small cloud the size of a man's hand was rising from the sea. Elijah told the servant to tell King Ahab to ready his chariot and flee; a storm was coming. As fast as the king's horses were, "*The power of the LORD came on Elijah and, tucking his cloak into his belt, he ran ahead of Ahab all the way to Jezreel*" (1 Kings 18:46 NIV).

Solomon encountered the power of the Lord in a most unique way. He was raised in the palace and was chosen by his father, King David, to take the throne after his death. (See 1 Kings 2:1–4). Solomon had some enormous shoes to fill in replacing his father as king. Not only was he challenged due to dysfunction in his family, but he was also tasked with the responsibilities and complexities of ruling a kingdom.

The Lord appeared to Solomon in a dream and said, *"Ask for whatever you want me to give you"* (1 Kings 3:5 NIV). Solomon replied,

> *"Now Lord my God, you have made your servant king in place of my father David. But I am only a little child and do not know how to carry out my duties. Your servant is here among the people you have chosen, a great people, too numerous to count or number. So give your servant a discerning heart to govern your people and to distinguish between right and wrong."*
>
> (1 Kings 3:7–9 NIV)

That very night, the power of the Lord filled him and made him the wisest man on earth.

JOHN WESLEY ONCE SAID, "BEAR UP THE HANDS THAT HANG DOWN, BY FAITH AND PRAYER; SUPPORT THE TOTTERING KNEES. HAVE YOU ANY DAYS OF FASTING AND PRAYER? STORM THE THRONE OF GRACE AND PERSEVERE THEREIN, AND MERCY WILL COME DOWN."[18]

---

18. John Wesley, *The Works of the Rev. John Wesley, A.M.*, vol. XII, 3rd edition (London: John Mason, 1830), 383, https://www.google.com/books/edition/The_Works_of_the_Rev_John_Wesley_A_M_Let/v-KxzQEACAAJ?hl=en&gbpv=1.

JUST FOR YOU...

You may already have some favorite Bible verses, but this one should be one of them: *"For God is working in you, giving you the desire and the power to do what pleases him"* (Philippians 2:13). Every once in a while, lay your hand on your heart and whisper, "Just as my heart is working in me, so is the power of God."

8

PRAYER STRENGTHENS YOUR FAMILY AND LOVED ONES

You are helping us by praying for us.
—2 Corinthians 1:11

The apostle Paul shared in a letter to the church in Corinth about the dangerous trouble he and his traveling party encountered on his journey through the province of Asia. "*We were crushed and overwhelmed beyond our ability to endure, and we*

99

thought we would never live through it. In fact, we expected to die" (2 Corinthians 1:8–9).

Over the course of the apostle Paul's missionary journeys, he survived being whipped with thirty-nine lashes on five different occasions, was beaten with rods on three occasions, pummeled with stones once, shipwrecked three times, and spent a whole night and day adrift at sea. (See 2 Corinthians 11:24–25.)

This amount of pain and suffering would break the frame of any man. The stature of the apostle was much smaller than most. He was four-foot, nine inches tall,[19] with a crooked body and a bald head.[20] He also had crooked legs, with eyebrows meeting, and his nose was somewhat hooked.[21]

Unlike many other places in the world, within the United States, there is very little physical punishment for being a Christian. However, no faithful Christian gets to live a life without scrutiny. Christians are the "most widely targeted"

---

19. Ferdinand Prat, "St. Paul," in *Catholic Encyclopedia*, vol. 11, ed. Charles Herbermann (New York: Robert Appleton Company, 1911).

20. Albert Barnes, *Notes on the New Testament: Explanatory and Practical, Vol. VI, Corinthians and Galatians* (New York: H. Franklin, 1840).

21. Abraham J. Malherbe, "A Physical Description of Paul," *Harvard Theological Review* 79, nos. 1–3 (1986): 170–75.

faith group in the world.[22] Those who condemn the Bible the most come from those who have read it the least.

Society allows and encourages all walks of life and frowns on anyone who disagrees with their choices. However, if you're a Christian, brace yourself; your faith will be cross-examined continually. Sarcastic comments and insulting smirks will be all too familiar. Condescending questions seem as if they could come from any direction. Even those who have no answer for the origin of life believe the Creator described in the Bible is outlandish and wrong. It is laborious and difficult to grip firmly onto faith.

TO CHOOSE TO LIVE FOR CHRIST IS TO CHOOSE TO LIVE A MISUNDERSTOOD LIFE.

As Paul and his men sat broken and weak, they found themselves remembering the power of God. Their moods, strength, and courage slowly rose as they relied on God instead of themselves. They put their confidence in Him to rescue them. And then Paul remembered that the believers who were a part of the church in Corinth were praying. Paul wrote a

22. Ewelina U. Ochab, "Recognizing the Phenomenon of the Persecution of Christians Globally," *Forbes Magazine*, November 30, 2019, https://www.forbes.com/sites/ewelinaochab/2019/11/30/recognizing-the-phenomenon-of-the-persecution-of-christians-globally/?sh=6c87cdfb3935.

message and sent it to them: *"You are helping us by praying for us"* (2 Corinthians 1:11). His words were an acknowledgment of how their prayers were working. They were also a passive request for them not to stop.

There are teachers, there are preachers, and there are comforters. The people are like angels walking among us who come in just the nick of time to make sure that, at our lowest points, we do not lose all faith. They're like paramedics who make our hearts brave. Blessed be the lifeguards keeping loved ones from drowning in the water of depression.

Have you ever found out that someone was praying for you? Did you not want to hug them and, from the deepest part of you, say thank you? Knowing how encouraging they were, ask the Holy Spirit to bring people to mind who need you to pray for them. Let them know so you may be the kind of friend we all need.

Our petitions to the Almighty are powerful enough to change the life of a loved one who isn't even praying for themselves. In the ninth chapter of the gospel of Mark, we read of a father who brought his demon-possessed son to the disciples to be healed. The demon would seize the boy and throw him violently to the ground. He would foam at the mouth, grind his teeth, fall into seizures, and become rigid. The demon would attempt to kill the boy by hurling him into the fire or into water. To make the situation even more awful, the evil spirit made him unable to hear and speak.

The disciples were unable to drive the demon out of the boy. A large crowd had now formed, and teachers of the law were arguing with the disciples. The father could have very easily lost all hope and returned home. But he was too desperate to give up. Many faint before they receive what they're asking for.

Jesus questioned the crowd about the commotion, scolded them for their unbelief, and told them to bring the boy to him. The father's halfhearted belief was met by Jesus's response, *"Everything is possible for one who believes"* (Mark 9:23 NIV). Isn't it true that it's easier to believe God will work a miracle in someone else's life than it is to believe God will work one in ours? The father responded, *"I do believe; help me overcome my unbelief!"* (Mark 9:24 NIV). Jesus rebuked the unclean spirit, *"'You deaf and mute spirit,' he said, 'I command you, come out of him and never enter him again'"* (Mark 9:25 NIV). The child didn't come to Jesus and ask to be healed. The father came to Jesus. The child couldn't speak, so the father spoke for him. The child had no faith, but the father did.

The time will come when you have a loved one in desperate need of a touch from the Lord. You may wonder if your prayer will make any difference at all. Scripture, the inspired words of God, assure you God is able to rescue, bless, and heal your loved ones even if they aren't praying for themselves.

I've been asked before if our prayers can go so far as to save a person. Every person must pray their own prayer of salvation, acknowledging Jesus Christ as their Lord and Savior. But your prayers are powerful enough to eliminate all the infliction and deception of the enemy and to remove the scales off their eyes so that they can clearly see the wonders of God. At that point, your loved ones are able to make an uninfluenced decision on whether they want Jesus to be their Lord. I have not met or even heard of anyone who, having once been blinded by the enemy, saw the Lord as He is and did not run toward Him.

THE BATTLE IS TOO DANGEROUS FOR BELIEVERS NOT TO INTERCEDE FOR ONE ANOTHER.

Satan orders the hosts of hell to fight against the children of God with great fury. It is around the standard bearers who refuse to follow the behaviors of this world that the battle is the hottest. If he can cut down the standard bearer, there will be no distinction between those who live for the Lord and those who do not. We all need a comrade.

I have a friend who is an evangelist, so he's constantly flying from one city to another, preaching at local churches. He told me that he was exhausted after service one night and, when he returned to his hotel room, was tempted to open his laptop and visit illicit websites. The enemy likes to attack us the most when we're tired. My friend reached out to his brother and said, "Pray for me. I'm weak right now." Consequently, he had the strength to endure the night without being overcome. Thank God he had a praying brother.

Around the age of twelve, my father went to New Mexico to preach to the Navajo people. He traveled around the country for several years, so this three-day, two-night trip didn't seem much different than any other. The first night he was gone, I awoke and, suddenly wide awake, got out of bed and laid face down on the carpet, pleading with the Lord not to allow my father to die. Tears were rushing out of my eyes. I was so scared that I'd never see my dad again. The next night, the same thing happened. Shortly after, I fell asleep, woke up, and prayed with unbearable anguish, begging God to keep my dad alive. Strangely, I knew it was okay to stop praying. I crawled back into my bed and fell sound asleep.

When my dad returned, he told me that he had forgotten the inhaler he used when his asthma attacks would occur. He said that each night, he'd lay on his back, and it felt like he was breathing through a small straw. I told him how I was waking up each night to pray passionately for him. He and I both knew that the Holy Spirit was waking me up to intercede for him. My prayers were the reason my father lived.

I had a friend named Jonathan who attended the same church as me in our teenage years. Jonathan was living a double life. The congregation knew nothing of how sinful he was living at night, and his friends had no idea he attended church regularly. His father was a man of prayer and lifted his name up before the Lord without rest. After one particular Sunday service, a woman in our church approached Jonathan and said, "I see a string around your neck holding a wooden board on your chest that reads, 'Sold Out.'" She explained that a day was coming when all would know that he would sell out and completely commit to the Lord. This seemed like a farfetched prophecy, but over the course of several months, Jonathan did indeed become one of the most passionate friends in my life for the things of God. Thank the Lord he had a praying father.

When Paul wrote, *"You are helping us by praying for us"* (2 Corinthians 1:11), he wasn't writing to just one person. The letter was to the entire church. There was a group of people who were coming together to pray for him. Unified intercession causes the power of prayer to multiply exponentially. It's a powerful thing when one person is banging on a door, but there is an accumulated force when two or three are banging the door together.

Wherever people are gathered together praying for one another, the embers of the Holy Spirit are in the air. These are the places where those who crave more of the power of God to be displayed in their life receive what they are asking for. The most powerful among us are those who pray.

JUST FOR YOU...

I have gone through seasons when I wondered whether anyone was praying for me. The Lord spoke to my heart one day and said, "If you take care of other people, I will send people to take care of you." I was so encouraged. I dialed in my focus to be a source of strength and encouragement. I smiled when the day came when I received an email that read, "I just want you to know I'm praying for you."

Ask the Holy Spirit to help you pray for others with the same passion you want others to pray for you.

Children return home with humble hearts. Husbands and wives lay down their swords and embrace. Your closest friends will not be able to resist the drawing of the Holy Spirit.

THERE IS NOTHING MORE POWERFUL IN THE WORLD THAN WHEN YOU LIFT YOUR VOICE IN PRAYER ON BEHALF OF YOUR FRIENDS AND FAMILY.

I have one more thought I want you to tuck into your heart: Jesus is at the right hand of God, and He is also interceding for you. (See Romans 8:34.) Think about that. Jesus is praying for you!

9

PRAYER REVEALS
THE UNSEARCHABLE THINGS

*Call to me and I will answer you and tell you great and
unsearchable things you do not know.*
—Jeremiah 33:3 (NIV)

We do not forget to eat. Our bodies order us to do so, and
we quickly respond. No one needs to remind us to reach for
a drink. Most of the human body—an average of roughly 60

percent—is water. If we want to live, we must drink. We are not forced to sleep; we know we must.

God says, *"Call to me and I will answer you and tell you great and unsearchable things you do not know"* (Jeremiah 33:3 NIV). He isn't asking us to call on Him; He is telling us to. He knows that if we don't, we will try to plan and strategize every part of our life all alone. If we take that route, we're going to feel like there are areas of our life we just can't seem to hold together. Our life will be riddled with frustration because it won't matter what we say or do; the most difficult areas of our life will either remain unchanged, or they'll dreadfully drag on far too long. Regardless of our weaknesses and inconsistencies, He's standing by, ready to be called upon.

Insurance companies are perplexing to me. I'm confident that if I were in the profession, I'd have far more understanding. I'm positive not all companies are this way, but the ones I've had experience with seem to have very little grace. I once read an illustration about how an insurance company cancelled someone's insurance policy after they had been in a car accident, and I laughed because the same thing happened to me.

I increased the insurance on my car in case I were to get into an accident. Unfortunately, I did get into a fender bender. The insurance company paid for the damage, and a few weeks later, they sent me a letter informing me that I was a high-risk driver, so they'd have to drop my coverage. I had to go to another insurance company to be insured. I never forgot how they were in my corner, receiving my monthly payments, until I had an accident.

The invitation God is laying before His children isn't available only if we're as pure as an angel. In fact, He tells us to look to Him because of His awareness of our distress and weakness, as well as the things that torment us. The Lord saw his prophet Jeremiah in such dire straits; He said to him, *"Call to me and I will answer you and tell you great and unsearchable things you do not know"* (Jeremiah 33:3 NIV.)

Scripture records that when God called Jeremiah to be a prophet, Jeremiah tried to decline by protesting, *"I do not know how to speak, for I am only a youth"* (Jeremiah 1:6 ESV). The Lord assured him that the right words would be placed in his mouth. The nation of Judah, where Jeremiah was sent, mostly ignored Jeremiah's warning, which caused him to mourn with many tears. His message to the people reads, *"But if you will not listen, my soul will weep in secret for your pride; my eyes will weep bitterly and run down with tears"* (Jeremiah 13:17 ESV). The grief he felt led to his being called "the weeping" prophet.

Difficulties and discouragements can make someone wish they had never even tried to share the treasure they had found. It would have been far easier if Jeremiah had resisted God's choice to live a secluded life. I believe the Holy Spirit spoke a word into Jeremiah's heart similar to Mordecai's words to Esther: *"For if you remain silent at this time, relief and deliverance for the Jews will arise from another place, but you and your father's family will perish. And who knows but that you have come to your royal position for such a time as this?"* (Esther 4:14 NIV).

When the Lord said to Jeremiah, *"Call to me,"* Jeremiah was under persecution. *"Now Pashhur the priest, the son of Immer, who was chief officer in the house of the LORD, heard Jeremiah prophesying these things. Then Pashhur beat Jeremiah the prophet, and put him in the stocks that were in the upper Benjamin Gate of the house of the LORD"* (Jeremiah 20:1–2 ESV). I'm sure there was a great deal of excitement when he first felt passion to be a witness, but now he feels as if he had been led astray. Lamenting, he writes, *"O LORD, you misled me, and I allowed myself to be misled. You are stronger than I am, and you overpowered me. Now I am mocked every day; everyone laughs at me"* (Jeremiah 20:7).

> **THE DIRECTIVE THE LORD GIVES, *"CALL TO ME,"* IS ATTACHED TO THE PROMISE, *"I WILL ANSWER YOU."***

We've all dialed someone's phone number when it's of utmost importance that we talk with them. As we listen, the ringtone continues on; we're saying to ourselves, "Answer. Come on; please answer." Sometimes they answer, and sometimes they don't. God is promising to answer you—not only to answer you, but to tell you about the unsearchable things.

Daniel discovered unsearchable things when he was able to interpret dreams. (See Daniel 2:24–45.) John discovered them when he *"looked, and there before me was an open door in heaven"* (Revelation 4:1 ERV). For Simeon, the moment came when he held baby Jesus in his arms and praised God for being able to look upon the Messiah. (See Luke 2:28–32.) No one can discover these unsearchable things on their own; these are secrets only God can reveal.

I have a friend named Lucas who has never been a creative person, but before he goes into business meetings, he always asks the Lord for innovative ideas. He tells me how some of the ideas that cross his mind are so out of the box he's almost embarrassed to mention them. He hasn't always depended so heavily on God giving him ideas, but ever since he has, he's become one of the most coveted advisors in his industry.

The most valuable of all unsearchable *things* is to receive a revelation about who God is. Isaiah tells us of his experience when he was brought into the throne room of God.

Attending him were mighty seraphim, each having six wings. With two wings they covered their faces, with two they covered their feet, and with two they flew. They were calling out to each other, "Holy, holy, holy is the LORD *of Heaven's Armies! The whole earth is filled with his glory!"* (Isaiah 6:2–3)

Seraphim angels have been circling the throne for an unmeasurable amount of time, calling out the words over and over again. How can they be excited to say the exact words they've said billions of times before? Every time these seraphim circle around the throne, they're seeing new and wonderful dimensions of God they've never seen before; it's like seeing an endless number of colors within a cloudscape. Heaven's angels were witnesses during creation. They were in awe as God created the stars and planets throughout the universe, forming innumerable galaxies, yet praised God, *"The whole earth is filled with his glory!"* (Isaiah 6:3). The earth is the only place the angels are referenced. Theologian N. Emmons said that angels "have discovered more of the glory of God in this world than in any other part of the universe."[23] Wise is the one who has no greater passion than to discover the depths of God.

The most precious of all unsearchable things is having the ability to be in the world but be so intimately aware of God that you can feel as though you're living in a suburb of heaven. The multitudes of people who followed at a distance didn't have the same experiences as the twelve disciples. The twelve disciples did not have the same experience as John when

23. N. Emmons, "God most fully displays his glory on Earth," Bible Hub, https://biblehub.com/sermons/auth/emmons/god_most_fully_displays_his_glory_on_earth.htm.

he laid his head on Jesus's chest. Though you haven't reached heaven yet, you live so close you can experience its glory.

There is a story in the Bible that illustrates this point very well. In Acts 16, we read about how Paul and Silas delivered a young girl from a spirit that enabled her to tell the future. This angered her masters, as she had earned them money by her fortune telling. The men seized Paul and Silas and brought them before the authorities. A mob grew in size against Paul and Silas, and the authorities ordered that they be stripped, beaten with rods, and thrown into prison.

About midnight, Paul and Silas started praising the Lord through prayer and the singing of hymns. What kind of relationship did Paul and Silas have with the Lord where they were compelled to sing in the midnight hours from a cold cell? The other prisoners did not have the same experience.

> PAUL AND SILAS WERE IN A CELL, BUT THEY WERE MORE AWARE OF THE PRESENCE OF GOD THAN OF ANYTHING ELSE HAPPENING AROUND THEM.

They were in the world but engaging in another world. All these things are too lofty to understand.

Centuries before, Enoch would walk on the same ground as all other humans, yet Scripture records that *"Enoch walked with God"* (Genesis 5:24 ESV).

In 1928, a lady named Kathryn Kuhlman started her ministry, which went on for five decades. She was known for hosting healing services with thousands in attendance in arenas and stadiums across the United States. During one particular service, she stopped speaking, covered her face in her hands, and sobbed. She looked up at the congregation and pleaded, "P-l-e-a-s-e. Please don't grieve the Holy Spirit." Still sobbing, she said, "Don't you understand? He's all I've got!" She continued, "Please! Don't wound Him. He's all I've got. Don't wound the One I love! He's more real than anything in this world! He's more real to me than you are!"[24] This type of relationship is reserved for all who pray.

---

24. B. Hinn, *Kathryn Kuhlman: Her Spiritual Legacy and Its Impact on My Life* (Nashville: T. Nelson, 1999).

JUST FOR YOU...

Let your imagination fuel your prayer life. The Lord tells you to call on Him because He longs to be just as close to you as anyone who has ever lived. The unsearchable things the Lord will reveal to you are more extravagant than any prize this world has to offer. Set for yourself a preplanned A-time, B-time, and C-time to spend time with God. You're A-time is the time you've planned to spend with God. If something comes up that keeps you from praying during your A-time, your B-time is your fallback slot to pray. If, once again, something comes up, your C-time is your safety net.

I was in a meeting with a friend when the alarm on his phone sounded. He informed me that he set multiple alarms throughout the day to stop for a moment to praise God. He didn't praise long, maybe three or four sentences that were something along the lines of, "Jesus, I love You so much, I thank You for all You've given me; mostly, I thank You for Your Holy Spirit that's with me now."

I encourage you to call upon the Lord often. Plan your appointments with the Lord. You will not have to covet other people's relationships; you'll take full joy in your own.

10

PRAYER BRINGS CONFUSION
TO YOUR ENEMIES

The LORD caused the warriors in the camp to fight
against each other with their swords.
—Judges 7:22

God chose Israel, out of all the people on the face of the earth, to be His people, His prized possession. They were a mighty nation until they refused to stop flagrantly sinning without

119

repentance. Consequently, God allowed the entire nation to be attacked and conquered by the Midianites. The prisoners of war began to cry out to God for mercy. As He is always faithful to do, He responded.

Find encouragement in knowing that during the seasons where you find your heart to be cold and your conscience seared, the moment you turn your face to the Lord and call upon Him, in less than a nanosecond, He forgives you and begins to move your life briskly forward.

An angel of the Lord came to Gideon and promised him that his troops would overtake the Midianites as if they were fighting against one man. (See Judges 6:16.) This word from the Lord contradicted all logic. The Midianites had an army of one hundred and thirty-five thousand soldiers. Gideon's army had been reduced from thirty-two thousand to three hundred. They were outnumbered four hundred and fifty to one.

Since Gideon had received a visit and message from the angel of the Lord from the courts of heaven, he was courageous and prepared for battle. (See Judges 6:34). However, his courage did not last for very long. Soon he began to second-guess the entire message relayed by the angel of the Lord.

Faith was pierced by fear. Devils promptly attack the moment the Lord speaks. Satan immediately sends birds to eat the seeds of faith that were meant to be planted in our hearts. Thorns grow quickly and sprout to choke out the promises given by the Lord. The enemy does whatever he can to cause us to second-guess what we were once sure of. As He is with each of us, the Lord was patient with Gideon when he asked for another sign to give him more assurance that his army would defy all odds and be victorious. We often look for guarantees that remove all fear. Faith gives us just enough confidence to be scared, yet believe in God anyway.

Seeing Gideon's panic rising on the night of the battle, the Lord persuaded him to spy out the Midianite camp. Gideon and his servant Purah were able to listen to a conversation between two Midianite men. We could imagine that they overheard the conversation the Midianite men had as they were sitting around a campfire. Or maybe Gideon and Purah listened through the thin fabric of their tent.

One soldier said to the other, *"I had this dream, and in my dream, a loaf of barley bread came tumbling down into the Midianite camp. It hit a tent, turned it over, and knocked it flat!" His companion answered, "Your dream can mean only one thing—God has given Gideon son of Joash, the Israelite, victory over Midian and all its allies!"* (Judges 7:13–14).

Imagine why God used a tumbling loaf of bread to illustrate how the Israelites would conquer the Midianites. In the dream, the loaf accomplished a feat disproportionate to its size. Dreaming of a boulder being fired out of a cannon and leveling the army's campsite would seem far more sensible. Yet, God portrayed Gideon and his army to be as strong as a loaf of bread. Only God Almighty would be able to receive the glory for their victory. They could not return to their families and speak of their heroics. The only thing to be said would be, "Look what the Lord has done."

A few years after our church had its very first service, a real estate agent called to inquire as to whether we were interested in purchasing a church building one mile away from the high school where we were meeting. We needed a building, but our small congregation could not afford to pay the mortgage of a multimillion-dollar building. We could hardly afford the lease for the school we rented one day a week. Our finances were as thin as a slice of cheese.

Real estate was in a downturn market, so our finance team decided to lob a Hail Mary proposal to the owners of the building, recognizing there was a tiny chance it would be considered. We believed the owners would laugh at our proposal, but we did it anyway. Surprisingly, they were open to negotiating terms. Conversations back and forth went on for months. During that time, our congregation experienced a substantial increase in attendance. We were still a small church, but our growth spurt was more significant than anything we previously experienced.

With the increased attendance, the business team saw that if we owned the building, we could handle the monthly cost. The mountain before us was the hundreds of thousands of dollars for the down payment required for purchase. We had a small fraction of the amount the owners were expecting.

The day came when the real estate agent told us that her client accepted all terms and we could move forward as soon as we made the down payment. Before we discussed the magnitude of their requirement, we laughed and shook our heads, amazed that they were open to selling to us.

We were far too small of a congregation to merit such a large facility. Our team joked with each other that, if we were to invite all of our members into the sanctuary, the empty space would be so large that we could drop a bus from the ceiling, and it wouldn't touch anyone. We could put a blindfold on each person and tell them to run around, and no one would bump into each other for hours. Nevertheless, saving enough money for the down payment would take us years.

Figuring it to be our last meeting with the seller before we parted ways, Chris, a gentleman on our business team, sent a message to the seller's representative saying, "We're ready to purchase the building, but we're not going to be able to offer a down payment. Cash flow is important to us." Our entire team nearly fell out of our chairs laughing. Of course cash flow is important to us—we didn't have any cash! His statement was hysterical.

A few days later, I received a phone call from Chris. He read the sellers' reply: "We completely understand how cash flow is important to you. The board members of our church have decided to sell you the building without a down payment." My eyes were as big as golf balls. "Are you kidding me? How in the world did they accept your comment, 'Cash flow is important to us'?"

I wanted to fly down the street and negotiate to buy a new car just to tell them I would not be giving a down payment because, "Cash flow is important to us." I made a note to myself: the next time I go to buy a house, I'll say, "I would give you a down payment, but cash flow is important to us."

After we had returned to our senses, we recognized that God had arranged for the breadcrumbs in our bank account to be enough to roll over our obstacles. Once we had a place to call home, our congregation started growing rapidly. Not many years later, we were able to pay off the loan so that our church building was completely debt free. Only God could hush all the thoughts the enemy was sending our way to discourage us from having just enough faith to keep moving forward.

Gideon bowed in worship before the Lord after hearing the dream and its interpretation. He raced back to the Israelite camp, gathered his three hundred men, and told them that the Lord had guaranteed their victory over their enemies. The Spirit of the Lord gave him a plan of action. He gave each man a ram's horn and a clay jar with a torch in it, and he divided the three hundred men into three groups. (See Judges 7:16.)

Gideon said to his men, *"Keep your eyes on me. When I come to the edge of the camp, do just as I do. As soon as I and those with me blow the rams' horns, blow your horns, too, all around the entire camp, and shout, 'For the LORD and for Gideon!'"* (Judges 7:17–18). Gideon's relaying God's instructions with clarity to his men and his men obediently following Gideon was crucial to ensuring victory over the Midianites. If we do not commit to following the ways of God, we are committing ourselves to failure.

After midnight, Gideon and his men reached the edge of the Midianite camp. With the camp surrounded, Gideon and his men blew on the rams' horns and broke their clay jars. *"They held the blazing torches in their left hands and the horns in their right hands, and they all shouted, 'A sword for the LORD and for Gideon!'"* (Judges 7:20). The Lord caused great confusion in the Midianite camp, and their soldiers fought against and killed one another with their swords.

Gideon's entire strategy was given to him while he was alone in prayer. If he would have just sat in his tent and wrung his hands together, he would have never been victorious. His army would have been led like sheep to the slaughter. The soldiers would have never again seen their wives, fathers, mothers, and children. His decision didn't affect just him; it involved hundreds of lives looking to him for leadership and comfort.

The entire narrative of Gideon defeating the Midianites is covered in only twenty-five verses. It's impossible to record every detail, including how scared Gideon and all his men were, and every other overwhelming challenge. One thing we can be sure of is that Gideon was a man with a nature just like ours. He had the same struggles we experience when we pray. The apostle Paul too speaks of wrestling in prayer. (See Colossians 4:12 NIV.)

I would fiercely contend that God didn't give Gideon every step of His plan the moment he began to pray. Just like the rest of us, Gideon's spirit was restless as he actively waited for the Lord to respond. To actively wait is completely different than simply waiting. Actively waiting is to continue in fervent, passionate prayer during the waiting. This is the way for all who call on the name of the Lord.

The one hundred and twenty believers waiting in Jerusalem day after day to receive a God-given promise to receive power were not just sitting on stools staring at the wall. They were praying as they waited. These disciples were facing a different type of enemy than Gideon. Their enemy included well over a thousand hecklers, laughing and hurling insults. Very quickly the Holy Spirit spun the crowd into confusion. They were bewildered because each of the believers were given the power to speak in their native language. (See Acts 2.) Just as God did with an ordinary man like Gideon, on that day, He used simple uneducated people to demonstrate the power of God.

Peter also capitalized on their enemy's confusion by preaching about who Jesus was, and on that day, three thousand people dedicated their heart to the Lord. (See Acts 2:41.)

Every time you pray, the Lord takes over the atmosphere, and devils are thrown into a spiral of confusion. All people who the devil is using to attack you will either have their hearts changed, or they will be escorted out of your life. The people who tolerate you will be replaced by people who celebrate you. You are born to war in prayer. Your destiny is to be lifted by the victorious right hand of God.

JUST FOR YOU...

In all the challenges that are sure to come your way, you will always be at least as strong as a loaf of barley bread. The enemies that come before you will be confused about how you, with such little strength, were able to overcome all their evil schemes.

"God chose things the world considers foolish in order to shame those who think they are wise. And he chose things that are powerless to shame those who are powerful" (1 Corinthians 1:27). God chose things despised by the world, things counted

as nothing at all, and used them to bring to nothing that which the world considers important. The only thing that matters is that the Creator of the universe, who governs the world, has delicately designed you and crafted your future; therefore, you are of great importance.

11

PRAYER TEACHES YOU HOW TO HEAR THE VOICE OF GOD

"Speak, your servant is listening."
—1 Samuel 3:10

There is an interesting correlation between drunkenness and prayer: just as alcohol can influence and control your thoughts, emotions, and decisions, so can the Holy Spirit influence you. In Acts 2, as the crowds witnessed the apostles and others praying in Jerusalem, they believed they were all drunk. Paul comments on being filled with the Spirit and contrasts it with being "*drunk with wine*" (Ephesians 5:18).

While Hannah prayed fervently with focus and passion, Eli, the chief priest, also presumed she was drunk. The Lord honored Hannah's prayer by giving her a son who would teach all generations about hearing the voice of God. (See 1 Samuel 1:12–17.)

Hannah's son, Samuel, was a miracle baby. He was the result of a praying mother. From the beginning, the child was dedicated to the Lord. It's never too early or too late for a parent to passionately persuade their children to be anchored in the church. Desiring to give God all she loved, Hannah handed her son over to Eli to live and to be mentored 24/7 in the temple of the Lord by the man of God. (See 1 Samuel 1:19–2:11.)

According to the first-century Jewish historian Josephus, Samuel was twelve years old the first time the Lord spoke to him.[25] The Lord said Samuel's name in the middle of the night while Samuel was fast asleep. The voice was so clear Samuel assumed Eli was calling him from his bedroom. "*So he ran to Eli and said, 'Here I am, for you called me'*" (1 Samuel 3:5 NKJV). He didn't disrespect the voice by ignoring it because he didn't want to crawl out of a warm bed. Nor did he take the

---

25. Flavius Josephus, *Josephus: The Complete Works*, trans. William Whiston (Nashville: Thomas Nelson, 2004).

words lightly by slowly walking toward Eli's bedside. Samuel ran down the hall. He wanted to be called upon because it made him feel valued and loved. In response, he greatly loved his father-in-the-Lord and devoted himself to his service.

Samuel was perplexed when Eli told him he had not called for him, so he needed to return to bed. A second time, Samuel heard the same voice call for him. Just like before, he rushed to Eli's bedside. Once again, Eli told Samuel that he had not called for him and told him to return to bed. A third time, Samuel heard his name. At this point, he must have felt that he was hearing things. Samuel was embarrassed to wake Eli again, but who else could have called his name? He tapped Eli's arm, but this time, the priest perceived it was the Lord speaking. He told Samuel that the next time he heard his name, he should respond by saying, *"Speak, Lord, for your servant is listening"* (1 Samuel 3:10 NCB).

"Now Samuel did not yet know the Lord: The word of the Lord had not yet been revealed to him" (1 Samuel 3:7 NIV). Therefore, Samuel was unable to recognize the voice of the Lord, but he was eager to learn. When he said, *"Speak, Lord,"* he started the conversation. If he had not responded, he would have never become the mightiest prophet of his generation.

If Samuel presumed that the voice he was hearing was from Eli, that would lead us to believe the Lord was not speaking in a booming voice. That's not how He talks to one of His children. Moses revealed what conversations with our Father are like when he said it's *"as a man speaks to his friend"* (Exodus 33:11 ESV).

Samuel could have easily brushed off what he was hearing because it was too familiar to be God. Yet Samuel's ears were listening. He was committed to learning how to identify His voice. We must not look past those moments when we think we have heard from God. Engage in the moment by saying, "I'm listening, Lord, speak to me." The conversation will begin with an exchange of thoughts at lightning speed.

If Samuel could have easily heard Eli's voice, then Eli may have heard the voice Samuel was hearing, too. Perhaps the voice wasn't out loud for all to hear; perhaps instead, as a loving father would not want to startle his son in the middle of the night, the Lord whispered, "Samuel. Samuel."

I have heard of people who have heard the audible voice of the Lord, and I believe them. I always talk with the Lord, and it's as real as anything I have ever experienced. He has given me many specific prophetic words for others, and it's never been audible. Like my friends in the ministry, the voice is as authentic as any voice, but it's always a flash of a thought. A whisper is so quick and so soft you could almost miss it.

I was talking to a friend the other day whose coworkers were saying horrible things about him to his face and behind his back. All the accusations were completely false, so he started to defend himself. It was one against ten. When they were all together, he'd focus on speaking to one person; the others would gang up on him. He told me he was praying for help while he was driving home from the office. In a flash of a thought, the Lord whispered, "Stay quiet. Do not defend yourself anymore." He knew beyond a shadow of a doubt he had heard the voice of the Lord. From that moment forward, when his coworkers criticized him, he'd say, "I hear you. I see your perspective." Soon his accusers could not use his words to fuel their fire. They ended up looking for something else to bicker about. The word of the Lord was a whisper.

Just as Samuel had to learn to distinguish the Lord's voice, we also have a trial-and-error process. The most consistent way you'll hear from God is to read what He's already said. If we value what the Lord has said, we'll quickly identify what He is saying. As you read, you may read for a good bit of time, but then there will be a moment when you know the words you just read are for you. It's a word written to answer and give direction for the exact situation you're experiencing.

A young person hears encouraging comments referring to potential and a bright future. As you get older, there is a point when people no longer mention your potential. I vividly recall a season of my life when I began to believe that I had come far short of reaching my potential and that my trajectory would remain as is without any reason to be excited about the future. I needed a word from the Lord. Learning to hear from God begins with studying what He has written.

I decided to open the book of Isaiah. *"It is too small a thing for you to be my servant to restore the tribes of Jacob and bring back those of Israel I have kept"* (Isaiah 49:6 NIV). The presumed plan for the servant of God was too small; the plan was far broader than anticipated. The things God said were far beyond what the servant imagined. I knew then that if I remained in prayer, I would walk through doors of opportunity I was unaware existed. That one word from the Lord gave me instant excitement about what lay ahead.

The activation of His promise would begin as I followed Him. God called me to be obedient to the slightest nudge of the Holy Spirit and to make prayer my highest priority. This lifestyle involved setting appointments to be alone on my knees in prayer. Equally as important, I'd pray throughout the day with more focus and intentionality. Doors of opportunity started opening—doors I could have never opened myself.

"Speak, your servant is listening." Those simple words lead to a peace that exceeds anything you are able to understand. (See Philippians 4:7.) Peace isn't an emotion—it's a place. Whenever you pray those words, "Speak, Lord," you begin to notice that peace in an unseen world becomes real in the place where you are. You learn to distinguish His voice from others in these unique places. It's almost as if the Lord surrounds you so closely you no longer feel the tension and worry.

C. S. Lewis put it this way: "If you want to get warm, you must stand near the fire: if you want to be wet, you must get into the water. If you want joy, power, peace, eternal life, you must get close to, or even into, the thing that has them."[26] A boy kept falling out of his bed. He called his mother and told her that his bed was broken. His mother said, "Your bed isn't broken. You're just not in deep enough."

Thank God for the soul's unrest; it causes us to pray. Prayer begins a conversation. The more you participate, the quicker you learn to identify His voice.

A person may say there was one time when they were sure the Lord spoke to them, but it's never happened again. Look back on that moment. What gave you such great confidence that God was speaking to you? Was it something you read? Was something spoken? Was it an emotion? A dream? Was it an epiphany? The way a person hears from God the first time is typically the way they hear His voice the most often. It's a decisive step when we say to the Lord, "In the same way You've spoken to me before, I'm asking for You to speak to me again."

I have learned that if we say to ourselves, "I'm going to start praying, but all I plan to do is praise the Lord for all I'm grateful for, and that's it," praising the Lord causes the Holy Spirit to make Himself known. It's fascinating how, after a period of praise, though it wasn't our original intention, we'll notice that the Holy Spirit will begin to guide our thoughts toward petitions. Identifying these transitions is to identify the Lord's

---

26. C. S. Lewis, *Mere Christianity* (New York: HarperCollins, 2001), 176.

voice. You'll feel compelled to start asking and praying about anything and everything.

Samuel's relationship with God grew to a place where he could receive a word from the Lord to amplify his own relationship with the Lord and hear about the future for others as well. Scripture encourages us to desire this gift of prophecy. *"Pursue love, and desire spiritual gifts, but especially that you may prophesy"* (1 Corinthians 14:1 NKJV).

Whenever someone came to me to say what the Lord had spoken to them about me, my heart would speed up because I was afraid that every wrong thing I'd ever done was about to be exposed. As I studied the pattern over the years, I discovered that it's exciting when someone shares what the voice of the Lord has told them because a prophetic word has particular characteristics. *"One who prophesies strengthens others, encourages them, and comforts them"* (1 Corinthians 14:3). As you identify the whispers and promptings from the Lord, He will give you things to say to strengthen others. When this happens, hurry to them to share the exciting news.

of love and mercy. It's never condemning. I've always uplifting.
They are the greatest moments on earth.

JUST FOR YOU...

How would you describe your prayer life? Would you say that it's nonexistent? Infrequent? Would you say that it's free-flowing and continuous? Is it a monologue or a dialogue? The relationship the Lord longs to have with you is to talk with you just as one talking with a friend. Don't pull away from learning to hear His voice. Each time you say, "Speak, your servant is listening," the conversation begins. For me, the words He always begins with are, "I love you." You may notice the same. You'll always know His voice because it's always full of love and mercy. It's never condemning but always uplifting. These are the greatest moments on earth.

12

PRAYER TURNS POOR DECISIONS INTO GREAT VICTORIES

The hair on his head began to grow again
after it had been shaved.
—Judges 16:22 (NIV)

Samson was born to be a champion. He was set apart to defend Israel and to destroy their Philistine enemies. From birth, he was to be a Nazarite. The vow of a Nazarite was to abstain from all things that come from a vine, including wine and grapes. Total abstinence from alcohol was required. In order to be set apart in every way, unable to blend in with the rest of the world, a Nazarite was never to cut their hair. Samson's lion-like mane, tied into seven braids, announced his allegiance to the God of Israel. God gave him a gift of supernatural physical strength so that he could fight victoriously,.

When a young lion came roaring toward Samson, the Spirit of the Lord entered him, and with his bare hands he ripped the lion's jaws apart. (See Judges 14:6.) He caught three hundred foxes, tied their tails together in pairs, and tied a torch between each pair of tails. He set the torches on fire and sent the foxes into the Philistine grain fields and olive orchards, scorching the entire harvest to the ground. (See Judges 15:4–5.) He used the jawbone from a donkey carcass to kill a thousand Philistines. (See Judges 15:15–17.) Samson once took hold of the doors of the city gate and the two posts, ripped them out of the ground, put them on his shoulders, and carried them to the top of a hill. (See Judges 16:3.)

For centuries artists have brushed paintings of Samson, showing his extraordinary feats of strength. In each, we see a man with massive muscles and a powerful-looking body. However, in Scripture, he was an average, ordinary-looking guy. He didn't have bulging biceps, a massive chest, or huge legs. Instead, his enemies were baffled because his physical appearance did not indicate that he had superhuman strength.

They were constantly asking each other what made him so strong. Samson's power came from no human source.

As strong as Samson was physically, he was weak morally. We read of how he'd fight against the Philistines, and then he'd feast with them. He lusted after their women. I once heard Glenn Burris Jr., a wise and seasoned minister, urge that there should be a watchful eye on three critical subjects: the gold, the glory, and the girls. Money is a good servant but a bad master. Forever lost is the person who's always looking for glory and admiration. If a woman isn't your wife, don't lust after, flirt with, or touch her. It was the third warning that Samson ignored.

Samson was involved with three Philistine women. The first was a woman from Timnah he wanted to marry. His parents objected. *"Isn't there even one woman in our tribe or among all the Israelites you could marry?' they asked. 'Why must you go to the pagan Philistines to find a wife?' But Samson told his father, 'Get her for me! She looks good to me'"* (Judges 14:3).

Imagine overhearing that conversation. "Yeah, Dad, I know I shouldn't be with her, but she looks good to me." As soon as the engagement celebration ended, she betrayed Samson by sharing the answer to a riddle that he posed to thirty Philistine men. He gave the men their prize for answering the riddle but was enraged by the situation. Samson returned home and lived with his parents while his wife married his best man. (See Judges 14.)You can't flirt with fire and not expect to get burnt.

> NO ONE WAKES UP IN THE MORNING AND SAYS, "TODAY IS THE DAY I'M GOING TO FLAGRANTLY SIN AND DO THE BEST I CAN TO MESS UP MY LIFE."

Devils are stealthy. They're experts on making sin appear to be a solution. The enemy tempts the angry, lonely, discouraged, and tired with evil solutions. We begin to believe that if we just do or say this or that, we'll have instant relief from our troubles. The enemy plays both sides of the line. Before you cross the line, he'll say, "Just do it. You'll feel better, and you deserve it. It's not that big of a deal." Once the line is crossed, he's there to say, "Look what you have done! Now you've made everything worse." Satan encourages you, and then he condemns you.

God set the same option before Samson as He does each of us. He could continue to go down his reckless path, or he could turn and instantly, without punishment, walk in a perfect relationship with God. The psalmist said, *"The sacrifice you desire is a broken spirit. You will not reject a broken and repentant heart, O God"* (Psalm 51:17).

Samson was unwilling to turn from a sinful nature full of lust and deception. He continued to take the bait the enemy set before him. After Samson regrouped from his deceiving fiancé, he went after another Philistine woman. Upon arriving in the city of Gaza, he met a prostitute and spent the night with her. (See Judges 16:1–3). The relationship only lasted a few hours but highlighted his poor decision-making. And then there was Delilah.

Some battles are sent to weaken us, and then there are battles sent to destroy us. There are poor decisions in Gaza, and then there are catastrophic decisions with Delilah. Everyone knows Delilah. It's the place where you were surrounded with only trouble and sorrow. It's the season of life you barely escaped. If you had stayed in that relationship or circumstance any longer, it would have broken you. Looking back, you can't help but shake your head, amazed by how God rescued you. Someone in our church once said to me, "If you knew what I've been saved from, you would understand why I worship the way I do." Love has no bounds toward He who has saved them from the deepest depths.

Samson followed Delilah like a sheep to the slaughter. Seduction was in her eyes, and lust dripped from her lips. People who entice you to indulge in flagrant sins do not love you—they hate you. Such tempters know that your decision could ruin everything you hold dear to your heart. Anyone who knows that and yet continues to persuade you hates you.

When the Philistine rulers found out Samson was in love with one of their own, they extended her an offer she was quick to accept. She'd receive 1,100 silver coins from each of the rulers if she could cunningly talk Samson into revealing the secret of his strength. (See Judges 16:5.)

Initially, Samson was able to withstand the temptation to risk it all. He tricked her on three different occasions regarding the secret of his strength. However, Delilah was relentless. *She tormented him with her nagging day after day until he was sick to death of it*" (Judges 16:16).

IF THE ENEMY CANNOT DEFEAT YOU TODAY, YOU CAN BET HE'LL BE BACK TOMORROW.

No one should be admired for having the ability to stand up to temptation but rather for their ability to run from it.

Samson confessed that if his hair were to be shaved, he'd lose his strength and be as weak as any other man. *"Delilah lulled Samson to sleep with his head in her lap, and then she called in a man to have off the seven locks of his hair"* (Judges 16:18). Samson awoke to Delilah's cries of a Philistine attack. He saw that he was surrounded. With a shaved head, he hurled his fists, but this time his punch had no impact. He found that his strength was lost. The Philistines captured him, gouged out his eyes, bound him in bronze chains, and locked him to a grain mill to work in prison. The Nazarite warrior became a clown in the eyes of the Philistine crowd. He was the spectacle of entertainment.

Samson's hair was not the source of his strength. His hair represented the covenant he had with God. Despite his propensity to sin, he kept his covenant. So long as he remained in covenant with God, he would continue to receive supernatural strength. The sheers not only cut his hair, but they also severed his covenant.

At the mill, locked in chains, Samson might have said, "Devil, you tricked me. You manipulated me. You exploited my weaknesses against me and kicked my legs out from under me. But you made a mistake—you counted me out while I still have breath in my lungs." The psalmist writes, *"I love the LORD because he hears my voice and my prayer for mercy. Because he bends down to listen, I will pray as long as I have breath!"* (Psalm 116:1–2). The Philistine may have shaved off Samson's hair, but the roots remained, and his hair began to regrow quickly.

Godly couples may have the enemy charge in and cut off all the flowers of a marriage, but there are roots too deep to sever. The Holy Spirit will cause the rosebuds to bloom again. The very moment husbands and wives begin to pray, roots begin to grow. They'll start leaving love notes for each other, squeezing their hugs tighter, and closing their eyes again when they kiss.

You may have a loved one who knows the truth but has become enchanted by sin. They have been caught in the devil's snare. The enemy has cut all that has braided their heart to the Lord. Every godly thing has been shredded. It seems as if there is no hope for such a cold soul. Take courage: the enemy may be able to cut all the threads that kept them closely knitted to the Lord, but he can't destroy the roots planted deep within their hearts. Fathers and mothers, pray on! Brothers and sisters, pray on! Dearest of friends, pray on! Don't ever stop praying. There is nothing on earth more powerful than prayer. At any moment, a touch of the Holy Spirit is able to cause those protected roots to grow again and return to their loving Savior.

After the Philistines cut Samson's hair, they stopped paying attention to him. It was foolish to think that his hair would not grow back. Samson may have rubbed his head to feel the growth of his hair. He may have smiled and thought, "Yes, it's all coming back. I'm still in chains, but my strength is returning." Let's all echo those words each time we're grinding at the mill. Say out loud, "Thank you, Jesus, for being right here next to me. You've never left me. I know You're making me stronger." The Philistines witnessed God's power but were unaware of His mercy and grace.

It's a wonderful thought to know that we do not need to figure out how to regain our strength. Strength is not something obtained instantly. You must consistently do something that builds your muscles. Don't worry about how you're going to regain your footing. Instead, stay laser-focused on cultivating your connection to the Holy Spirit. Your victory is in His hands. At just the right moment, the Lord will show His strength.

The Philistine rulers held a great festival honoring and praising their god because Israel's champion Samson had been defeated and become their slave. Over three thousand Philistines filled the temple and temple roof during the festival. The people demanded, *"Bring out Samson so he can amuse us!"* (Judges 16:25).

> IGNORE THE JEERING THOUGHTS OF THE ENEMY. HE HAS A LONG HISTORY OF CELEBRATING BEFORE THE END OF THE STORY. HE NEVER ANTICIPATES HOW QUICKLY GOD RESPONDS TO THE FIRST CRY FOR HELP.

Samson asked the servant leading him by the hand to *"Place my hands against the pillars that hold up the temple. I want to rest against them"* (Judges 16:26). If you kneel before God, you can stand before any man.

Your story is an intricate part of God's story. Our daily battles are not between us and Satan; they're between God and Satan. Satan cannot touch God, so he aims to kill His children. Every time the Lord steps in and delivers us from our trouble, He receives glory, and the devil scampers away like a wounded beast. Every demonic grip loosens when we call on the Lord during adversity.

Samson prayed, "*Sovereign* LORD, *remember me again. O God, please strengthen me just one more time. With one blow let me pay back the Philistines for the loss of my two eyes*" (Judges 16:28). Samson pushed against the temple pillars praying a final time, "*Let me die with the Philistines*" (Judges 16:30). The temple collapsed on all the Philistines in attendance at the festival. In his final act, Samson "*killed more people when he died than he had during his entire lifetime*" (Judges 16:30).

Samson's most significant victory wasn't before his greatest mistake but after. The prayers he prayed during his lowest moments led to his greatest victory. No decision we make nullifies the Lord's ability to use us in mighty ways. The only determining factor is whether we have the fortitude to look up while we're down. Our Father in heaven will continually "*strengthen you and help you. [He] will hold you up with [His] victorious right hand*" (Isaiah 41:10).

JUST FOR YOU...

You also are a Samson. You've done some extraordinary things. You could never recount all the people who have looked at you and said, "Thank you." There is no such thing as a small act of kindness. Every expression makes an indelible impact. Some moments cause a brief spark of happiness that make smiles. Other things you've done and said are so special they'll never be forgotten. Can you recall a few of those moments?

You are also a Samson for another reason. You are able to do more with the rest of your life than you have thus far. I have learned that the more we pray, the more confident we become that things that lie ahead of us are more significant than the things that are behind us. As we pray, we will receive a greater anointing and greater favor with both God and man.

13

PRAYER CHANGES THE ATMOSPHERE

When Solomon finished praying …
the glorious presence of the LORD filled the Temple.
—2 Chronicles 7:1

There is a particular store at the mall I will not enter ever again. As a teenager, I used to collect posters of my favorite basketball players and hang them on the wall in my room. I'd heard that this particular store had a variety of posters toward the back, and many of them were basketball players. The moment I stepped in, I felt an unsettled and icky feeling that I didn't have before I walked in. It was dark in the store, and the items being sold were provocative. The graphics on the T-shirts were vile. There was something evil in the atmosphere. I left the store, and I've never returned.

> We are not fighting against flesh-and-blood enemies, but against evil rulers and authorities of the unseen world, against mighty powers in this dark world, and against evil spirits in the heavenly places. (Ephesians 6:12)

Now that I have children of my own, I've told them never to enter the store either. I was proud of them when they looked through the window and said that they wouldn't want to go in there anyway. The apostle Paul reminded the church in Ephesus that Satan is *"the mighty prince of the power of the air"* (Ephesians 2:2 TLB). Satan fights to establish his presence wherever he can gain a foothold.

Many of you have noticed that there are certain places where you consistently feel heaviness or despair in the air. In these spots, the battle is the hottest. Here there is a heightened temptation to engage in bitterness, rage, anger, harsh words, and slander and to feed addictions, lust, and many other types of luring behaviors. If you study the lives of Gideon, Job, Paul, Peter, and Esther, as well as many other great men and women of God in the Bible, you'll see that they also had to fight unseen spirits hovering in the atmosphere. Paul said to Timothy, *"I have fought the good fight"* (2 Timothy 4:7 ESV). As previously mentioned, he was fully aware that he wasn't fighting against people. The good fight was against the prince of the air.

Solomon shifted the atmosphere to be exclusively reserved for the Holy Spirit. Solomon's temple was the first temple built by the Israelites to honor God, and it was more exquisite than any person had ever seen. It was ninety feet long, thirty feet wide, and forty-five feet high. The temple was built from masterfully quarried stone blocks, with a roof and interior lined with cedar beams and planks. Solomon used pure gold to overlay the temple's holy inner sanctum, placing a pair of fifteen-foot-tall angels made with wild olive wood and overlaid with gold to guard the ark of the covenant. No hammers, chisels, or iron tools were heard at the temple site during construction; any stones used were finished at the quarry. (See 1 Kings 6.) The temple was a most holy place and must have been a sight to behold.

Solomon gathered the elders of Israel, heads of the tribes, priests, and people of Israel for the Festival of Shelters. King Solomon and the people of Israel sacrificed numerous sheep, goats, and cattle. The priests carried the ark of the Lord into the temple's inner sanctuary. As the priests exited the inner sanctuary, an unimaginable event occurred. The Spirit of the Lord appeared in a cloud and rested in the atmosphere. The priests fell to the ground.

Imagine the overwhelming awe each person felt when the cloud filled the temple. How did they respond when the source of all power invaded the room? They were unable to stand, and the place was too solemn, too holy to utter even one word. Some experienced perfect peace, while others wept for joy. God had filled the house.

All of this took place the moment they started to worship. The psalmist writes, *"But thou art holy, O thou that inhabitest the praises of Israel"* (Psalm 22:3 KJV). The Hebrew word for *inhabit* is *yeshiva,* which means "to dwell." This historic moment reveals to us that when our praises go up, His presence comes down.

> WHEREVER YOU BEGIN TO PRAISE THE LORD, WHEREVER YOU ARE—WHETHER IN YOUR HOUSE, CAR, OR OFFICE—YOU'RE SURROUNDED BY THE ALMIGHTY GOD.

Scripture goes on to say that when they worshiped, they raised their voices and said, *"He is good! His faithful love endures forever!"* (Psalm 136:1). The children of God didn't merely sing a song; they raised their voices. James tells us that fervent prayer is the kind of prayer that causes the greatest impact. (See James 5:16.) If we're going to be passionate about anything, let us pray and worship with passion. The stakes are high enough to offer nothing less. Nowhere in Scripture can we find a warrior praying casually. Instead, we read of hands and voices being raised. Initially, choosing to be this type of worshipper can be uncomfortable. It's a significant step to move toward putting some fervor into your praise. You can have comfort, or you can have growth, but you can't have both.

The cloud of glory did not just hover above the roof of the temple. It filled the room. As you praise the Lord, you do not need to worry about any other spirits. The prince of the air must submit to the Alpha and the Omega. *"This is what the LORD says to you: Don't be afraid or discouraged by this great army because the battle isn't yours. It belongs to God!"* (2 Chronicles 20:15 CEB).

I have a habit of handling problems head-on. If someone is causing me stress, I quickly have a conversation and seek a resolution. I do not like unresolved conflict. I've often been guilty of rehearsing my words in my mind in preparation for the upcoming discussion. Admittedly, rarely has anything good come out of these meetings. Most of the time, I've only made the situation worse and caused the awkwardness to last far longer than it should have. I'm embarrassed to confess that I once suggested to one of our children that they must not hesitate to immediately confront the friend who was the source of their problems. It was humiliating when the reply was, "I don't feel good about that. I believe if I pray, God will take care of this for me." I was so humbled. I apologized immediately for giving such poor counsel. Sure enough, the situation was resolved, and there were no residual effects. Our victory will come "'not by might nor by power, but by my Spirit,' says the LORD Almighty" (Zechariah 4:6 NIV).

The manifestation of the power of God when you pray and worship cannot be predicted. It can be tangible, as described above, or you can have a keen sense of knowing that the Divine has taken complete dominion in your space. However, you can be sure that when God steps in the room, He always brings joy. Rightfully so, joy is often linked with laughter, as it is a common way the Lord replaces grief with gladness. (See Psalm 30:5.) We must also be aware that the depth of joy has multiple expressions. In its truest form, joy brings pleasure and happiness. I know the presence of God is in the atmosphere when I start noticing and enjoying all the incredible things I've been given that I'm prone to ignore.

Time spent with family and close friends results in some of the most cherished moments in life. The chaos of this world causes us to take for granted what's most important to us. Joy highlights these treasured relationships and puts them in their rightful place in our life. Additionally, you become grateful for all the things money could never buy.

Some fears make us better human beings. They can cause us to work harder, be more diligent, and urge us to protect the most priceless things. This welcomed fear heightens our senses and keeps us from being reckless.

I had the opportunity one summer to ride a motorcycle. While the experience was exhilarating, it also had its share of fears. Riding fifty-plus miles per hour on an open road can be scary, especially if you dare to look straight down at the road speeding by underneath you. This type of fear is a gift because it causes you to be cautious. You can see the smallest debris on the road even if it's far ahead.

On the other end of the spectrum, there is also a spirit that arrives with tormenting fear. Paul writes to Timothy, *"For God has not given us a spirit of fear"* (2 Timothy 1:7 NKJV). This kind of fear causes a sustaining dread and angst. This spirit does not remain in a specific place; it clings to someone. Wherever they go, whatever they're doing, they're tormented by this spirit. It causes them to be distant, discouraged, downhearted, melancholic, overwhelmed, irritable, and tired. This spirit is so stealthy, one could almost believe that this is normal. Consequently, the unique nuances of their personality that make them attractive and fun to be around are suppressed. Over time, their life-giving personality and the warmth in their eyes and in their smile are no longer what people expect to see.

In contrast, Paul tells us the Lord provides us with a spirit *"of power and of love and of a sound mind"* (2 Timothy 1:7 NKJV). The wonders that take place when we pray and worship are endless. Paul writes to the church in Thessalonica, appealing and compelling them to *"Never stop praying"* (1 Thessalonians

5:17). He knew that *"the angel of the* LORD *encamps around those who fear him, and he delivers them"* (Psalm 34:7).

Oswald Chambers said, "The remarkable thing about God is that when you fear God, you fear nothing else, whereas if you do not fear God, you fear everything else."[27]

The most free-flowing, heartfelt praises often feel repetitive because you may realize you're saying the exact words over and over. For example, "Jesus, I love You. I love You. I love You." Or "I praise You. I praise You. I praise You." If each time you say those words, you are focused upon Him, then each time you say them, He will hear you as if it's the first time. The Holy Spirit will confirm within you that this is true by how close you feel to the Lord as you become an instrument of praise. The dwelling of God around you isn't something that comes and goes. It's meant to remain. Your simplest words cause you to live a life so blessed you can hardly explain it.

27. Oswald Chambers, *The Quotable Oswald Chambers* (Grand Rapids: Discovery House Publishers, 2011), 142.

JUST FOR YOU...

A close friend called me to tell me that he suspected an evil spirit was in his house because this was the only place where he felt overwhelming worry, grief, and heaviness. He assured me not to worry because he took care of it already. He told me that he opened the door and yelled, "Devil, get out of my house!" Then he began walking into every room in his house, lifting his hands, praying, and worshiping the Lord. He said, "The entire atmosphere of my home has changed!"

Never forget that your prayer and worship are immeasurably powerful. Out of all of God's creation, you are His prized possession. (See James 1:18.)

14

PRAYER RENEWS A LOYAL SPIRIT

Create in me a clean heart, O God.
Renew a loyal spirit within me.
—Psalm 51:10

David's father, Jesse, established God as the center of their family. Early on, there was a loyalty in David's spirit that kept him from drifting away while he led his father's sheep to green pastures and still waters. The Lord sought a man after his own heart to be the king of Israel after Saul. Under the Lord's guidance, Samuel anointed David to be the next king of Israel.

David was still a teenager when God plucked him from the fields and placed him in the palace. When King Saul was being overtaken by a tormenting spirit, David would come to play the harp, and every evil spirit would immediately be dispelled. He was *"a skillful musician, a mighty man of valor, a warrior, one prudent in speech, and a handsome man, and the* Lord *was with him"* (1 Samuel 16:18 NASB1995).

After Saul's reign, the Lord established David as the king of Israel. More has been written about David than any other biblical character. Sixty-six chapters are dedicated to him, and there are fifty-nine references to him in the New Testament.[28] *"David did what was right in the eyes of the* Lord *and did not turn aside from anything that he commanded him all the days of his life, except in the matter of Uriah the Hittite"* (1 Kings 15:5 ESV). This was the one matter where he laid his loyalty aside.

The downward spiral began while he was walking on the roof outside the chambers of his palace. His palace was at the city's highest point, and he was able to overlook the homes below. One day he noticed a beautiful woman bathing outside on her patio. He found out her name was Bathsheba, and she was married to Uriah the Hittite, a soldier in his army. David sent for her by messenger, and he slept with her when

28. "David: The Man After God's Heart; 1: A Heart of Hope," Bible.org, https://bible.org/seriespage/4-david-man-after-gods-heart-1-heart-hope.

she arrived at the palace. Some time elapsed, and Bathsheba discovered she was pregnant and sent David a message alerting him.

David attempted to cover his tracks by bringing Uriah home from the war to sleep with Bathsheba, but Uriah was more concerned with the war and his men than taking pleasure in his wife. David then devised a plan to have Uriah placed on the front lines of the battle where the fighting was the most intense. As a result, Uriah and several other Israelite soldiers were killed. Bathsheba mourned Uriah's death, but David sent for her to be one of his wives after the mourning period ended. (See 2 Samuel 11.)

LUST AND DECEPTION WILL TURN US INTO A PERSON WE NEVER THOUGHT WE WOULD EVER BECOME.

Sometime afterward, the Lord sent the prophet Nathan to David to deliver a message. He told him a story of two men who lived in a certain city. One was rich, and the other was poor. The rich man had many sheep. The poor man had only one, but he loved her as one of his own children. He allowed her to drink from his cup and eat from his plate. One day the rich man had guests coming to visit, so he planned to prepare a meal. Not wanting to slay one of his own sheep, he took the poor man's only sheep, killed it, prepared it, and served it for supper.

When David heard this, he went into a fit of rage. "'*As surely as the LORD lives,*' *he vowed,* '*any man who would do such a thing deserves to die! He must repay four lambs to the poor man for the one he stole and for having no pity.*' *Then Nathan said to David,* '*You are that man!*'" (2 Samuel 12:5–7).

David had sinned against God. His heart was torn, and his spirit was crushed. He cried to the Lord, saying, "*Oh, give me back my joy again. You have broken me*" (Psalm 51:8). If you've ever felt close to the Lord, even once in your life, you're familiar with the sadness that comes when that closeness is interrupted. David was pleading for his sins to be blotted out. He had sinned against God, and it was haunting him day and night. His sorrow and shame were a burden too heavy to bear. "*When I kept silent, my bones wasted away through my groaning all day long*" (Psalm 32:3 ESV). The mental anguish marred his face. He had always protected his relationship with God, but when he saw Bathsheba, his loyalty was no more.

My friend Jackson had felt the hollowness inside that comes from feeling distant from God. He told me of the day he decided to draw a line in the sand and leave the past behind to learn to host the presence of God. After a few weeks, he realized he could hardly watch any TV or movies because nearly every time he was in front of a screen, he'd see something risqué. In his heart, he knew that those moments grieved the Holy Spirit. He was not willing to allow any entertainment to interrupt his intimacy with the Lord, so he made a sacrifice to protect his relationship with God. The things that entertain us will soon consume us. David took pleasure in watching Bathsheba, but that wasn't enough; he had to have her, whatever the cost.

Longing to reestablish the joy he once had, David looked to the Lord and pleaded, *"Create in me a pure heart"* (Psalm 51:10 NIV). David was wrestling. He longed for God, but he lusted after sin. David had wine for communion in one hand and the forbidden fruit in the other. In most cases, when someone has unrighteousness and righteousness warring in their soul, they stop praying. Not David. Though he was tempted to withdraw and go silent, he called for help: *"Unseal my lips, O Lord, that my mouth may praise you"* (Psalm 51:15).

IF THE ENEMY CAN KEEP US FROM PRAYING, HE CAN GAIN A FOOTHOLD IN OUR LIFE.

The enemy will try to seal your lips by telling you lies—like that your disobedience is unpardonable, your heart has gone cold, and your life is too sinful. David knew these thoughts were not from God. David praises the Lord by saying, *"You will not reject a broken and repentant heart, O God."* (Psalm 51:17) Repentant hearts have always been and will always be irresistible to God. Quicker than you can blink, you are forgiven.

The enemy will try to convince you there is no reason to pray because God does not exist. Charles Spurgeon said, "Atheism is a strange thing. Even the devils never fell into that vice."[29] Knowing silence is a trap, David declared, *"I will bless the LORD at all times: his praise shall continually be in my mouth"* (Psalm 34:1 KJV). In the middle of the turmoil, David chose to renew his loyalty through his worship and began drawing near to the Lord.

"Draw near to God, and he will draw near to you" (James 4:8 ESV). At first glance, it appears that this verse should have been written in the reverse order. It seems like God would draw near to us first. This particular verse was written for those who are as desperate as the woman with the issue of blood: she didn't wait for Jesus to draw close to her but went to Him to receive her healing. (See Luke 8:43–48.) This verse is an invitation; the Lord is saying, "If you want me, come! Every time you take a step toward me, I'll take a step toward you." God bids us to come to Him freely, and He'll embrace us, not unlike a child seeking and receiving the warm embrace of their father.

---

29. Charles H. Spurgeon, *Spurgeon at His Best: Over 2200 Striking Quotations from the World's Most Exhaustive and Widely-Read Sermon Series* (Grand Rapids: Baker Publishing Group, 1988).

The wonderful thing about this verse is that the sovereign Lord is asking you to take the initial step of drawing near, yet He is the one drawing you. Your desire to be close to Jesus is proof that God is calling you. Jesus said, *"For no one can come to me unless the Father who sent me draws them to me"* (John 6:44).

As a teenager, I could play basketball for hours upon hours, from sunrise to sunset, whether with friends or alone. I'd often lose track of time and forget when I was supposed to come home. My dad had a very unique, extremely loud whistle. I believe if I were at the top of the highest mountain, I could still hear the sound that could have only come from him. I knew that when I heard his whistle, it meant he wanted my attention, and, in most cases, he was telling me that he wanted me to come home. Straight away, I'd start walking toward our house, but I wouldn't have if he didn't first call me.

Drawing near to God begins with thinking about God. I have a pastor friend named Joshua who went to visit his parents during an exhausting season of his life. He was sitting at the kitchen table with his mom, lamenting about how distant he felt from the Lord. As moms often do, she comforted him by patting his hand and telling him that this too would pass. His father was sitting in the living room and overheard the discussion. He came into the kitchen, sat down, and took a more direct approach. He asked Joshua if he had been reading his Bible regularly. Joshua confessed that he hadn't. His dad asked if he was reading any Christian books to be inspired.

Again, the answer was no. The next question was whether he had been listening to and watching recordings of other preachers. Joshua continued to say no. With love, yet firmness, his dad said, "Joshua, no wonder your thoughts haven't been on the Lord, no wonder you feel distant from the Lord, you're not doing anything to draw near to Him."

If we are not deliberate about filling our minds with the things of God, the things of God will not cross our mind. We must establish uncompromising, purposeful habits, such as making sure that worship music is playing in our vehicles and in our homes. We need to recognize the impact that takes place when we're in the house of God every Sunday, hearing the Word of God. Watching services online rather than going to church should be an option only exercised when you are not able to attend. The easy, most convenient path is rarely the most beneficial. There will always be sacrifice attached to sparking an acceleration. Each day, we are riding on the momentum created the day before. The reason you wake up with the Lord on your mind is that He was on your mind the previous day.

All of David's victories, even the one where he needed to reestablish his loyalty, were a result of his drawing close to the Lord. He stopped to praise the Lord seven times a day, and he prayed three times a day. (See Psalms 119:64; 55:17.) Regardless of whether you're on the mountaintop or in the valley, worship anyway. Our Lord is well aware that our flesh is weak. Nevertheless, "*As a father has compassion on his children, so the* LORD *has compassion on those who fear him; for he knows how we are formed, he remembers that we are dust"* (Psalm 103:13–14 NIV). Our God is *"Tenderhearted, kind, and forgiving. He has a thousand ways to set you free"* (Psalm 130:7 TPT).

> IF YOU COMMIT TO BEING A PERSON OF PRAYER, DON'T WORRY ABOUT BRINGING RESOLUTION TO THE CONFLICT THAT SURROUNDS YOU. GOD WILL BRING HEALING AND RESOLUTION IN A WAY THAT YOU WILL FIND TO BE GOOD, PLEASING, AND PERFECT.

JUST FOR YOU...

People may be able to out-sing you, but they cannot out-worship you. You're a born worshipper. People may be more eloquent than you, but they cannot out-pray you. The enemy flees, and his schemes fall apart when you lift your hands and your voice to the Lord. Prayer is your strength, and intimacy is your destiny. Do not let the enemy exaggerate your weaknesses and minimize your strengths. He may come in as a flood, but the Lord will put a wall up before him and say, "You cannot come any closer." Your assignment can only be completed by you, and it's never too late to become more effective and cover more ground than you ever have. The Holy Spirit within you is greater than any dark spirit around you. *"Hold up the shield of faith to stop the fiery arrows of the devil. Put on salvation as your helmet, and take the sword of the Spirit, which is the word of God"* (Ephesians 6:16–17). *"Be strong and courageous! Do not be afraid or discouraged. For the* LORD *your God is with you wherever you go"* (Joshua 1:9).

ABOUT THE AUTHOR

Houston native Frankie Mazzapica is the founding and lead pastor of Celebration Church of The Woodlands, Texas. Three people from the community were in attendance on the day that Frankie and his wife Allie launched the church in 2005.

Today, Celebration Church is a vibrant, multiplying community of believers. People experience a demonstration of God's power in the form of physical healings, changed lives, emotional restoration, and deliverance. Celebration's momentum and footprint continue to expand rapidly with multiple in-person services and a vast array of attention-grabbing digital platforms. Frankie's encouraging, challenging, and humorous messages are nationally broadcast each Sunday on TBN.

Frankie's conviction is that Jesus's three-year ministry, where teaching and miracles attracted seekers and built disciples, is the model for today's church. Believers should not rest until the same power displayed in the life of the Lord's disciples is present in their lives. Frankie's mission statement is, "I live to walk with the Lord and share His love and His power."

Ignite Your Life: 14 Powerful Things That Happen When You Pray is Frankie's second book. He wanted to share fourteen powerful things that happen when you pray to make an impact for God's kingdom. His first book, *Your Divine Invitation*, includes practical steps every believer can take to position themselves to receive God's promised endowment of power.

Frankie and Allie were married in 2001. They have two girls and one boy: Preslee, Luke, and Kate. They love the blend of urban and suburban life in The Woodlands, but they've built their home a half-hour away in the country, where one can see the shooting stars in the Texas night sky.

To connect with Frankie, visit:

Facebook: @PrFrankieMazzapica
Instagram: frankie.mazzapica
YouTube: FrankieMazzapicaNOW
TikTok: frankiemazzapica